winter
GARDENING

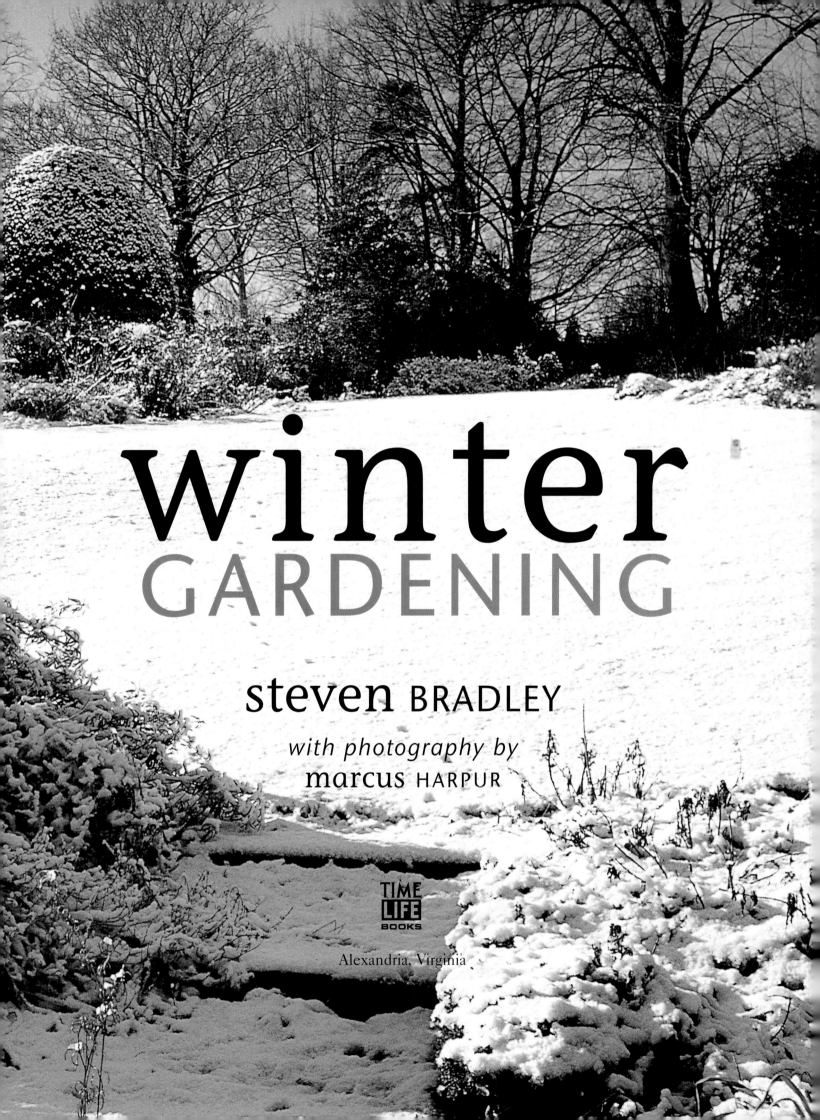

winter
GARDENING

steven BRADLEY

with photography by
marcus HARPUR

TIME
LIFE
BOOKS

Alexandria, Virginia

contents

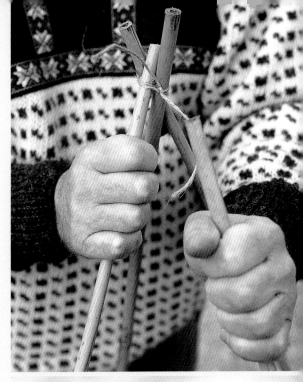

introduction

Winter, on the face of it, appears to be a quiet time in the garden, but it is just as important as any other season of the year. It is all part of nature's balancing act, with the visible part of the plants giving the appearance of being dormant, although there is usually a great deal going on inside roots and stems. It is easy to forget this fourth season of the gardening year. All too often, the winter quarter is dismissed as a "dead" time in the garden, yet it can be a time of varied activity and intense interest. Throughout spring and summer, plants grow steadily to store food and produce flowers and seed, and much of the year's activity is focused on these two busy periods.

The winter months can be a time for both reflection and planning in the garden, assessing the good and bad points of the past year, building on the successes, and making adjustments to those plans or schemes that were not quite as fruitful as was hoped. A busy winter may hold the key to gardening success in the coming season, and although the weather conditions may not seem conducive to outdoor activity, there are many gardening tasks that are far better done at this time of year than any other. An experienced gardener will see the cold weather as an ally rather than an opponent, using the right conditions to move or replace plants, or improve a difficult soil while the plants rest.

Winter gardening is not just about work—there are many plants that produce their best display and fragrance through the short days of winter. The colored stems of trees and shrubs can provide a glow of color against a dark background of evergreens, or an attractive tracery of shades highlighted by winter sun and a clear blue sky. Hips and berries add interest and activity as birds and small mammals visit the garden to feed on the fruits.

The winter cold usually causes a reduction in overwintering pests and diseases, with aphid eggs providing food for birds, and fungal spores being killed by the cold and wet conditions. This helps cut down infection levels on plants the next spring, reducing the reliance on chemicals to control many of the common afflictions on treasured plants. Many plants perform better after a cold winter, as low temperatures promote chemical changes in the plants, which appear to encourage stronger growth and better fruits and flowers the next year.

OPPOSITE *The bright* Mahonia x media *'Winter Sun' produces fragrant yellow flowers in early winter.*

ABOVE *The vivid red stalks of ruby chard create a splash of color in the winter vegetable garden; this makes an excellent winter crop.*

RIGHT *In winter you can see the garden in its most basic structure, and it is therefore an invaluable time for garden planning and design.*

BELOW RIGHT *A birdhouse provides vital cover and protection from wind and snow for birds in winter, or birds may seek shelter in winter foliage.*

BELOW *Topiary will look effective in any winter garden. The shapes and forms will be further enhanced by a dusting of snow.*

leaf
FALL

Fall is a time of gradually shortening days and lowering temperatures. These changes are recognized by plants at the beginning of winter, and their response is to become "hardy," so that as the temperatures continue to fall, the plant is able to cope and survive. This process, known as acclimation, usually occurs in two distinct stages.

The majority of plants depend on day length to control their "body clock," so that both longer and shorter days trigger changes within the plant, including the production of new growth, formation of flowers, and an increase in food storage. From mid- to late September, the days become short enough to bring about progressive changes within plants, leading to gradual preparation for dormancy and tolerance of sustained periods of cold weather.

Leaf fall actually starts earlier, when the plant first detects that the hours of daylight have become shorter than a set period of 12 hours within the 24-hour cycle. As part of this gradual process, the leaves of woody deciduous plants change color, from green through a range of red, yellow, and orange shades. This, the first stage of acclimation, happens as sugars, proteins, and nutrients are withdrawn and taken back into the woody tissues of the plant, for storage over winter and for use during growth the following year.

The second stage of acclimation occurs when the early frosts influence changes in the levels of proteins and sugars inside the woody tissue. This, in turn, helps to increase the plant's tolerance to cold temperatures. Even the hardiest of plants are unable to survive freezing temperatures without injury if they do not experience this two-stage process of acclimation. The degree of tolerance to low temperatures increases as the process of acclimation progresses into fall and winter, from a tolerance to temperatures of 23°F (-5°C) in late fall to an ability to withstand temperatures as low as -22°F (-30°C) by mid- to late winter. How well a plant can cope with winter cold will be influenced by the time of year when the severe weather begins, the stage of acclimation reached at that time, and the plant's innate hardiness.

RIGHT *During fall, some plants such as this* Acer palmatum *display vivid color changes, through greens and yellows to bright red.*

a time of transition

The season of fall derives its name from the fact that this is the time when leaves are shed by deciduous climbers, trees, and shrubs. Before the leaves are actually discarded, they undergo a number of color changes. In the north of the United States, this color change travels south at a rate of about 35–45 miles (60–70km) a day and is so pronounced that it can be detected from space. The progress of seasonal change is mirrored in northern Europe as well, with severe conditions and rapidly dropping light levels being most prevalent the farther one travels north.

ABOVE *During fall, even the shed leaves will be used by the plants, as they gradually decay and replenish the nutrients in the soil around the plant's roots.*

In some plants, the color changes of the fall leaves are slow and subtle, while in others, the changes are much more pronounced and vivid, to the extent that, for some species, this can be the most colorful and attractive season of the year. Most leaves are shaded green through the spring and summer, but this chlorophyll masks the many different types and quantities of pigment that are responsible for the colors of these leaves as they die.

As fall progresses, a major recycling process begins as the plants take useful nutrients from the leaves back into the stem and branches. These are stored over winter for use during the major surge of growth in springtime. Chlorophyll is the first pigment to be withdrawn from the leaf, which means that other pigments are left visible, such as red and orange carotene, yellow xanthophylls, and/or reddish purple anthocyanin pigments, which are the result of sugars building up in the leaves rather than being transported into the woody tissues of the stems and branches.

The richness and variety of the color display will vary according to the weather conditions being experienced during the period when the leaves are slowly dying. The ideal weather conditions for a good show of leaf color are a cool, damp fall, with very little wind or frost, as these conditions give slow color changes, with the leaves hanging on the plants for the longest possible time.

Once the plant has drawn as much from the leaf as it possibly can, the connecting veins linking the leaf to the stem are closed and sealed by the plant. A layer forms across the cells, effectively isolating the leaf, and acting as protection against water and harmful organisms entering the plant through these veins. The leaves will then fall from the plant within a few days of this abscission layer forming. This process, whereby plants "toughen up" in order to withstand low winter temperatures, is known

Factors such as temperature variations, or changes in the availability of water, vary greatly from year to year. They are less consistent than changes in day length over a one-year cycle, so for any plant a change in day length is a more reliable warning of the approach of seasonal changes to come.

Preparation for winter

It is not just the leaves that are undergoing changes in preparation for winter. Other, less noticeable (but equally important) changes are also taking place, which will help the plant as a whole stand a much better chance of coming through the cold period unharmed.

The shortening days stimulate a modification of some parts of the plant to provide protection for delicate areas, such as shoot tips and flower buds, so that they can emerge unharmed the following spring. Woody shoots gradually stop growing and those leaves nearest the tip of each shoot produce very small, thickened modified leaves, called leaf scales, which wrap tightly around the buds to protect them.

Deciduous plants effectively shut down during the winter months as a self-preservation mechanism. Their leaves are not frost-hardy, and therefore they would suffer severe damage as a result of exposure to low temperatures. The lack of leaves also helps to prevent the loss of water from the plant during the winter period, when the soil temperature is low and the plant would find it difficult to take up more water. This is why some conifers and other evergreen plants may develop brown leaves during the winter when they are unable to replace moisture that is lost in cold, windy weather.

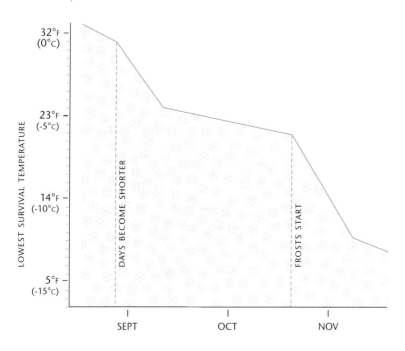

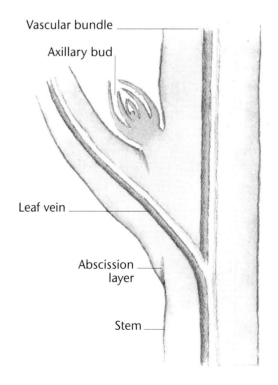

However, as with most rules, there are likely to be exceptions, and the fall coloring and shedding of leaves is no different. It is not just restricted to deciduous woody plants; even a small number of herbaceous perennials, such as the water dock (*Rumex hydrolapathum*) and a number of hardy euphorbias and geraniums, will show attractive foliage colors during fall. Unusually, several conifers also shed their leaves after a stunning fall display, including larch (*Larix*), the dawn redwood (*Metasequoia*), and the swamp cypress (*Taxodium*).

Unfortunately for the gardener, it is not just hardy plants that shut down for the winter. A range of pests and diseases also prepare to survive, ready to emerge the following spring. Common pests such as aphids will lay overwintering eggs in the fall, with toughened shells adapted to cope with winter conditions. Many familiar fungal diseases, such as rusts, develop toughened spores that survive the winter on dead plant material. Mildews infect the overwintering buds of the host plant and take advantage of the plant's protective coat to rest and survive, ready to reinfect the new growth the following spring as the soft, new (vulnerable) leaves emerge.

We may not realize it, but the garden never actually sleeps. There is no period within the year when there is nothing happening out there. At times, the activity may be minute, very gradual, or happening underground so that it is not easily visible, but nevertheless, it is happening. The plants need this resting period, of simply "ticking over," if they are to produce healthy growth and flowers the following growing season.

In fact, this period of low temperatures is often as essential for the general health and well-being of plants as water and sunshine are; without the chemical changes that will only occur in the plants while temperatures are low, a large number of the plants that normally grow outdoors in our climate would eventually die. Just the effects of chilling at temperatures between 36°F (2°C) and 28°F (-2°C) can be enough to bring about certain changes within the plant and can provoke it into the final stages of flower formation and bud development, or encourage seeds to emerge from their dormant sleep. These changes can occur at higher or lower temperatures, but the plant's response is often the most rapid in chilling temperatures rather than freezing conditions.

RIGHT   *Many types of climbing plants and wall shrubs will thrive when growing against a wall, as they benefit from the residual warmth from the sun radiated by the wall.*

investing in a winter garden

The "winter garden" is simply the garden in winter—one of the four seasons, which is a stage the garden will go through whether the gardener likes it or not. Bearing in mind that winter is also a time when the weather will be unpredictable, and it may be difficult to work outside, the aim of any gardener should be to make the garden as attractive and interesting at this time of year as any other.

ABOVE *Some trees and shrubs, such as this* Salix alba var. *vitellina 'Britzensis', will only be noticed after the leaves have fallen to expose the colored bark.*

OPPOSITE *Despite their lack of height and delicate appearance, winter-flowering bulbs are among the toughest of all the plants we grow in our gardens.*

There will still be plenty of work to do—in fact, winter can be one of the busiest and most rewarding times of the year in the garden, especially if there is any design or redevelopment work to be done. When the weather is really bad, time need not be wasted because there is always plenty of planning to do—figuring out how to improve the overall performance and the pleasure to be had from the garden, and how to benefit from it, not just in winter, but throughout the year.

Color

Any gardener who really gives the winter period some thought, and adopts a positive attitude toward it, will soon realize that it is a time of opportunity. The unique feature of the winter garden is the low temperature, and rather than seeing the cold and frost as an enemy, there are situations where it is possible to use a plant's response to cold to full advantage. A framework of evergreen and coniferous plants can help provide the basis of a permanent structure in the garden. Attractive shapes and distinctive color variations can be used to create subtle changes and variations. Even variegated evergreens, which have color throughout the year, look better in winter. The gold or silver patterns on the green leaves are more noticeable when neighboring deciduous plants have lost their leaves and offer less distraction to the eye.

Some plants that look rather ordinary for most of the year really come into their own when temperatures drop close to or below freezing. The foliage of the Japanese cedar (*Cryptomeria japonica*) turns a beautiful red-bronze in winter; many forms of the evergreen herbaceous perennial elephant's ears (*Bergenia*) adopt red tints to the margins of its large, almost circular, leaves; and the leaves of blood grass (*Imperata cylindrica*) turn flame-red when the weather goes cold. These plants only draw the eye and become really noticeable in the cold winter months, when they respond to the low temperatures and reward the gardener with a colorful display.

ABOVE The colored bark on the red stems
of Cornus *spp.* and white arching branches of
Rubus *spp.* provide an attractive splash of
color throughout the winter months.

BELOW *The shapes and silhouettes of plants
have a use. The old seed heads of plants such
as teasel (Dipsacus) will provide interest
during the winter frosts.*

Structure

Other plants may have more than one season of interest, with flowers
or foliage throughout the summer and characteristics that only become
distinctive in winter when the leaves have been shed, such as twisted or
contorted shoots. These bare stems will look spectacular against the blue sky
on a sunny winter's day. The corkscrew hazel (*Corylus avellana* 'Contorta')
has wonderfully twisted stems and produces golden yellow catkins before the
leaves emerge. There are a whole range of willows (*Salix* spp.) and dogwoods
(*Cornus* spp.) that are renowned for their brightly colored red, yellow, or
orange stems. *Salix* 'Erythroflexuosa' has the best of both worlds, with
brightly colored, orange-yellow twigs that are also spirally twisted, creating
even more interest. Other plants have the added bonus of variegated leaves,
which look equally attractive in summer and winter.

A thick riming of winter frost can make even dead plant material look
attractive. Plants where the top dies off, such as bamboo, grasses, and
herbaceous perennials, look stunning if the old stems are left in place until
spring. Plants such as angelica, hydrangea, ornamental onions (*Allium* spp.),
and pampas grass (*Cortaderia*) all have distinctive flower heads that persist
long after the flowers themselves have died, and look stunning when coated
in thousands of sparkling white ice crystals. In fact, leaving the flower heads
in place has a very practical application for the gardener, as they will absorb
the cold and help protect the remainder of the plant from frost damage.

TOP *The yellow, spiky flowers of* Mahonia x media *'Lionel Fortescue' will attract interest due to their strong scent as well as their attractive, brightly colored flowers.*

ABOVE *The tomato-shaped hips and veined leaves of the Japanese rose,* Rosa rugosa, *look attractive with a coating of morning frost.*

Fragrance

An additional bonus to the senses during the winter period is the number of scented plants that are in flower at this time. Perhaps it is the lack of competition, or the quality of the crisp, clear air, or both, but the scent given off by flowering plants at this time of year can be truly unforgettable. The evergreen mahonia, for example, has large, tufted trusses of sulfur-yellow flowers, with a scent reminiscent of lily of the valley, but much stronger. Another evergreen, elaeagnus, has strongly scented but well-hidden white flowers, which often leave the gardener looking around to trace the source of this delicate perfume.

Deciduous plants producing frost-hardy but strongly perfumed flowers on bare woody stems in the depths of winter include tough characters such as witch hazel (*Hamamelis*), the aptly named wintersweet (*Chimonanthus*), three varieties of winter-flowering bush honeysuckle (*Lonicera* spp.), and several daphnes for the smaller garden or front of a border. For more details on winter fragrance, see pages 106–11. Try to allow plenty of room between strongly scented plants to avoid a potential clash between fragrances.

Fruits

Fruits are also more noticeable in winter, when they seem to glow with color. On evergreens, such as firethorn (*Pyracantha*) and holly (*Ilex* spp.), the red, orange, or yellow berries contrast perfectly with the plants' glossy foliage, especially when the base color is dark green. Where the stems are bare, the clusters of berries are even more obvious, as with the brilliant purple of the beautyberry (*Callicarpa*).

The range of fruit colors can be both extensive and long-lasting, especially if a little care is taken when selecting the plants. Barberries (*Berberis* spp.) produce fruits colored in shades of orange and red through to velvety black. Cotoneasters produce berries of pink, red, or golden yellow. The hawthorns (*Crataegus* spp.) may bear orange, red, or golden yellow fruits; the different rose species have hips in shades from orange-red to bluish black. Possibly the widest range of colors is found among the mountain ash family (*Sorbus* spp.), with shades of red, yellow, orange, pink, and white berries.

Not only do these plants add a splash of color to the garden, but they also provide food to attract a host of birds and mammals. The antics of these visitors often gives as much pleasure as the plants themselves (see pages 130–9). For some plants, such as the spindlebush (*Euonymus alatus*), the brightly colored casings that hold the fruits will remain on the plant long after the fruits have been devoured by birds and mammals.

Winter favorites

The lack of leaves and herbaceous vegetation in the winter means that much more of the soil's surface is exposed to view. This is not a disadvantage, more an opportunity, as many small but attractive plants that would go unnoticed at other times of the year are easily seen in winter.

Plants that dislike a warm or shaded environment also come into their own at this time of the year. For the gardener this can prove useful, as these plants will flower in the dead of winter and will then vanish beneath the soil for the rest of the year, to emerge again the following winter. For some strange reason, many of the smallest plants we grow—often those with the most delicate appearance—are among the most hardy and come into full growth when many of their larger, bolder counterparts are dormant and sheltered from the elements.

Although winter-flowering bulbs are usually much smaller in flower and stature than their later-flowering relatives, most are strong and vigorous and capable of withstanding extremes of cold down to -10°F (-23°C). Even

though the individual plants are not large, they can produce a wonderful display when massed together in grouped plantings. At times it appears unbelievable, even to an experienced gardener, that such small plants can emerge and produce attractive flowers through soil covered with frost, or poke their heads through a layer of snow into the winter sunlight. The golden, buttercup-like flowers of winter aconite (*Eranthis hyemalis*), or the white bells of snowdrops (*Galanthus* spp.), are a welcome sight in any garden in midwinter, and a definite reminder that the garden is not asleep, merely resting.

If you look carefully, it is possible to find a few perennials that look their best in winter, including the large, tough leaves and pink flowers of elephant's ears (*Bergenia*), and more notably, the hellebores (*Helleborus* spp.). Indeed one, *Helleborus niger*, is even known as the Christmas rose. With its evergreen foliage and cup-shaped flowers, in colors ranging from green, through whites and pinks, to almost black, this plant seems to ignore the cold weather to flower. However, the older leaves can start to look very jaded in periods of prolonged cold.

In order to create and maintain an attractive and productive garden, some work will inevitably need to be done in winter as preparation for the coming seasons, including cultivation, pruning, planting, propagation, and harvesting. This being the case, it is far better to undertake these tasks in colorful and pleasant surroundings, with plants flowering or looking attractive in another way. Investing time and money in a winter garden makes the gardener want to be outside whatever the season or weather!

working winter diary

The onset of winter provides a variety of tasks for the gardener. Listed here are a number of jobs that the gardener can map out for the maintenance of the garden, as it is prepared for the coming of spring.

GARDEN AREAS	LATE FALL/EARLY WINTER		MIDWINTER	
TREES, SHRUBS, AND CLIMBERS	Plant bare-rooted deciduous trees and shrubs (including deciduous hedges and roses) • Root-prune new roses when planting, but do not prune	the top-growth until the spring • Established roses may be topped now; long stems can be shortened to reduce wind rock • Check and replace	plant supports as necessary • Start to take hardwood cuttings of strong-growing climbers and wall shrubs (continue through to March)	During milder weather, check tree-ties and replace rotten stakes • Firm trees showing signs of wind rock • Knock heavy falls of snow off densely branched shrubs
BULBS, CORMS, AND TUBERS	Plant bulbs, such as hyacinths, lilies, and tulips • Lift, dry, and store gladioli • Lift dahlias when blackened by	frost • Cut down the stems, and place the tubers upside down to dry • Examine lifted dahlia tubers for rotting •	Dust healthy tubers with sulfur and box up in dry peat or sawdust • Put in a cool, frost-free place	Bulbs that were grown in pots and have finished flowering can now be acclimatized in the cold
LAWNS	Continue to rake up fallen leaves regularly to reduce the chance of moss becoming	established; add the leaves to the compost heap or use to make leaf mold • As the	growth rate of the grass slows down, cut higher and less frequently	Lay new turf during mild weather • Overhaul mower and sharpen blades; check
POND MAINTENANCE	Cover the pool with fine mesh netting if falling leaves are a problem, to reduce any chances of the fish being	poisoned • If the submerged water pump is removed for winter, test it, then clean, dry, and lubricate it • Divide and	replant waterside plants • Thin out congested and submerged plants, especially those that die back during winter	If the pool freezes for more than a week, thaw a patch by resting a bottle of hot water on the ice to maintain
VEGETABLES	Lift potatoes, beets, and carrots for storing • Tie onions in ropes as soon as the bulbs are thoroughly ripened. Tidy up the vegetable plot, removing all debris • Sow	fava beans and hardy peas in the open—protect with cloches in cold areas • Remove dying leaves from winter greens to allow air to circulate freely between	the plants • Continue to check stored vegetables—remove all specimens that show the least sign of decay, putting aside those only slightly infected for immediate use	Plan next year's rotation of vegetables and a seed-sowing schedule for vegetables and flowers • Lift and store rutabagas and late-sown carrots • Lift a small quantity of vegetables, such as celery, leeks, and parsnips and
FRUIT	Continue to pick apples and pears, and check fruit in store. Remove any showing signs of rotting • Cut down old fruited blackberry and hybrid berry canes, and tie in young canes • Continue to order any trees,	bushes, or canes needed for winter planting • Prepare planting sites as necessary • This is a good time to plant fruit trees, bushes, and canes, although if the soil conditions are suitable, planting can be	carried out throughout the winter • Rake up and burn all diseased leaves • Newly planted fruit trees will require formative pruning • Check tree-ties and replace rotten stakes	Continue to prune established apple and pear trees in mild weather • Continue planting fruit trees if the soil conditions are right • Vigorous, unproductive fruit trees may be root-pruned now • Remove roof netting from the fruit cage if
GENERAL GARDEN	Clean and sterilize pots and trays • Tidy up herbaceous borders—dead stems may be left for added frost protection • Rake up leaves regularly • Burn diseased plants • Cut down stems of	chrysanthemums; lift and place the stools in boxes of compost or peat and place in a cold frame or cold greenhouse • Apply slug pellets, well-weathered cinders, or coarse grit around	the base of plants such as delphiniums, lupins, primulas, pyrethrums, and *Iris unguicularis* if slugs are troublesome • Clear and tidy up around the garden • Store equipment for winter	Order seeds • Complete digging, but do not work on wet soil • On clay soils, spread sand, old potting soil, or well-rotted leaf mold and dig in as soon as conditions are favorable • If the ground is frozen, wheel manure and compost onto undug plots •
GREENHOUSE/ SUNROOM	Replace shading with insulating plastic • Harvest green tomatoes and store in the dark to ripen • Clear growing bags and plant with winter lettuce,	strawberries, or spring-flowering bulbs grown for cut flowers • Bring in pots of bulbs after a spell in the cold frame. For a succession of flowers, leave some of the	bulbs in the cold frame for another two weeks • Lift, and place in the dark, crowns of chicory, rhubarb, and seakale, intended for forcing • Pot on pot plants for spring flowering	Clean the greenhouse • Destroy plant debris • Sow radish and carrot in growing bags or border, and lettuce for growing on under cloches • Prune grape vines
PESTS AND DISEASES	Continue spraying to control black spot and mildew on roses • Spray peaches and	flowering almonds to protect against peach leaf curl disease		Apply a winter wash (tar oil) to rid trees of overwintering eggs of pests if not already done • Spray

and conifers • Remove all dead, diseased, and untidy branches • Firm anything that has been loosened by wind or frost, and stake if necessary • Move deciduous shrubs if not	too wet • Renew neglected hedges of yew and privet by cutting one side back severely (cut the other side back next year) • Prune wisteria shoots back to two or three buds	Prune, feed, and mulch roses and shrubs • Move and replant shrubs before they break into full growth • Prune shrubs grown for winter bark effect, for example *Cornus*	and *Salix*, cut down to 6in (15cm) • Remove dead branches from early-flowering shrubs, such as *Hamamelis*, immediately after flowering • Prune climbing roses	• Cut back fall-flowering clematis (*C. texensis* and *C.* 'Jackmanii' types) to 1ft (30cm) above ground level • Plant new roses, shrubs, and hedging plants
frame before planting out • Check stored bulbs and corms and throw away any that are soft or diseased	• Order summer-flowering bulbs and store in a frost-free place	Protect crocus from marauding sparrows with netting or by suspending strands of cotton	over the flowers • Remove any dead flowers, so that the food reserves build up for next	year's flowers, and apply a general fertilizer • Plant gladioli corms
cables and connections on electric mowers • Avoid walking on the lawn	in frosty weather or when the ground is frozen or waterlogged	Lay turf in mild weather • Prepare ground for sowing grass seed • Scatter worm casts with a broom before	mowing • Do not walk on the grass when it is covered in frost • Watch your feet—it is easy to damage naturalized	bulbs emerging through the lawn • Make the first cut with blades set high • Lightly roll new turf, if lifted by frost
a breathing space for fish • Save a concrete pool from cracking by floating a plastic ball on the surface during icy	weather. If the pump has been left in the water, run it briefly every week to prevent it from silting up	If the pump has been left in the water, continue to run it briefly every week to prevent it from silting up • Service the pump if necessary • Lift, divide, and replant aquatics in	containers (not wood or metal). Covering your arms with petroleum jelly helps keep out the cold and makes washing easier • This is a good time to start constructing a	new water feature, if you do not already have one in your garden, while the soil is dry and firm
store under cover in a cool, accessible place if heavy falls of snow or prolonged frost are forecast • Sow fava beans, early peas, and spinach • Sow early maturing cabbage and cauliflower in pots • Place main-crop potatoes in shallow trays indoors • Sow cabbage,	carrot, lettuce, and radish under cloches or plastic • Sow salad onions in a growing bag under protection • Sow seed of beets, carrot, cabbage, lettuce, and peas (main crop) • Plant onion sets • Sow herbs	Sow fava beans, early peas, and spinach • Sow early-maturing cauliflower and cabbage in pots • Place main-crop potatoes in shallow trays indoors but protect from frost	• Sow cabbage, carrot, lettuce, and radish under cloches or plastic • Sow salad onions in a growing bag under protection (to get an early crop when they are	expensive in the shops) • Sow seed of cabbage, lettuce, peas (main crop), beets, and carrot • Plant lettuce under cloches or plastic • Plant onion sets • Sow herbs
heavy snow is forecast, and replace it immediately after risk of snow has passed • Cover strawberry plants with a cloche or low plastic tunnel for an early crop • Apply lime to the fruit plot if the soil is below pH 6.7 • Cut all newly planted	raspberries down to 9in (23cm) and all established canes to ground level • Apply fertilizer to fruit trees, bushes, and canes • Apply an organic mulch 4in (10cm) deep • Inspect fruit in storage and remove any that are beginning to rot	Plant rhubarb and strawberries • Feed established strawberries with potash and cover with cloches or plastic to get early fruit • Tip canes of summer-	fruiting raspberry cultivars. Cut fall-fruiting cultivars to ground level • Finish pruning apples, pears, and soft fruit • Plant apples, pears, and soft fruit • Finish pruning plums,	gooseberries, and red currants • Apply a nitrogen feed to black currants • Complete mulching of fruit • Train and tie canes of blackberries
Finish lightly forking over borders, leaving the soil surface rough • Sharpen, clean, and polish garden tools • Clear out the potting shed; scrub clean used plant labels and dirty pots for further use • Clean spraying equipment • Clear land-drain outlets and	open ditches • Give extra protection to crops under cloches if severe frost is forecast • Treat fences and other wooden structures with preservative • Lay out apple prunings to feed rabbits—this will help prevent them from damaging the trees	Fork over herbaceous borders • Plant *Crocosmia* and apply a general fertilizer • Sow late-flowering sweet peas *in situ* if soil is not too wet	• Continue digging as the soil conditions allow • Plant overwintered sweet peas outdoors • Mulch beds and borders while the soil	is moist to reduce watering and weeding later in the season • Prune roses before the year's new growth is well developed
• When the foliage has expanded and flower buds are visible, bring forced flowers indoors • Water plants as required—avoid overwatering • Remove faded	flowers and leaves • Remove plants from window sills at night and during freezing weather • Move potted bay trees to a frost-free position	Place dahlia tubers in pots or boxes of compost to promote early growth, but keep frost out • Sow geranium and begonia seeds • Watch for an increase in aphid populations,	particularly on cinerarias and calceolarias, and spray as necessary • Sow seed of summer bedding plants • Take cuttings of geraniums or buy new "plug plants" as	they come into the garden centers • Provide shade for houseplants with large leaves as they often wilt in full sun • Liquid feed the plants once a week
peaches and flowering almonds against peach leaf curl • During dry, still, frost-free weather, spray apples,	cherries, peaches, plums, pears, gooseberries, grape vines, raspberries, and currants with a tar oil wash	Start a spraying program to control fruit pests and diseases • Spray roses against black spot after pruning	• Spray cherries, peaches, and flowering almonds against peach leaf curl	

designing a
WINTER GARDEN

Whether or not weather patterns are changing, people are now spending more time outdoors enjoying the garden. As more of us spend our days working in air-conditioned offices, with a relatively sedentary lifestyle, the craving to feel close to nature is likely to increase. This will not only influence the type of garden we choose, but also the amount of time we spend in it.

Over the past few years, garden design has become as fashion-led as clothes and interior design, to the extent that the most publicized exhibits at leading flower shows have been submitted by fashion, rather than garden, designers. Plants and colors come into favor for a while and are then discarded for the new up-and-coming trends and styles. This may work with inanimate objects inside a house, but a garden is a living, developing place that deserves a longer-term plan. It should be designed according to your individual needs and lifestyle because you are the one who will live with it.

Not all trends are ephemeral; garden lighting, for example, has become popular with many gardeners, and although originally intended for creating an atmosphere in the garden on a summer evening, lights make a vast difference to the garden in winter as well, when the weather dictates that we sit inside, looking out. They add an extra sparkle to frost-covered plants and lawns and pick out the tracery of a tree's leafless branches. Lights are also useful for watching nocturnal wildlife feed, especially elusive visitors such as foxes or badgers. There are also practical uses for garden lighting: Low-level lights can be used as markers along pathways and well-positioned spotlights can be directed downward to reveal steps for safety purposes.

The beauty of this type of consideration when planning a winter garden is that use of the garden is immediately extended beyond the limitations of daylight hours. Above all, remember that a garden will never look exactly the same twice. It is a living, evolving entity, which will change and mature and in which flowers and leaves will come and go. Planning and designing the garden are just the first tentative steps along this evolutionary path.

RIGHT *The cold frosty mornings of winter highlight plants and garden features that go unnoticed at other times of the year.*

planning and design

When planning any type of garden, not just a winter garden, it is advisable to follow a few basic guidelines. Not only will this make life easier when designing and implementing any changes, but it will also help avoid disappointment later on when it will be much more difficult to change course.

Take the time to assess your requirements and to decide exactly why the garden, or part of it, is being developed. There might be a single reason; for example, to provide winter interest, to attract wildlife, or to reduce future maintenance levels. However, it is most likely that you will want to build all-year interest and several functions into the design at the same time.

Make a list of exactly what you want from your garden, writing it down so that you have a clear idea of how you will use the garden. This is especially important if you are developing the garden over several years rather than in one hit. Keeping a record is an effective way of keeping to a theme and making sure your good ideas are not lost, or even worse, remembered when it is too late to implement them because there is no room left. Be aware of all the things that have to be incorporated into the garden

BELOW *Plants and garden ornaments can be used as focal points to draw the eye to predetermined spots in the garden. The aim is to draw the visitor farther into the garden.*

area, such as a compost heap, and of how you will access them. Perhaps the greatest challenge of all is to create a garden with all-year interest, so that at least one (and preferably many more) plants are producing a display of flowers or some other form of seasonal interest for every day of the year.

PLANNING TO SAVE TIME AND WORK Planning ahead when redesigning a garden can reduce time spent in the completed garden on all those fiddly little jobs that seem to take forever and are usually the boring maintenance tasks that we would rather not perform.

A mowing strip of bricks (or narrow paving slabs) around the perimeter of the lawn will save days over the gardening year by eliminating the need to trim the edge of the lawn with a half-moon tool three or four times a year, and the need to trim the edges with a string trimmer after mowing. It also stops the edge of the lawn being shaved as the mower tilts over into the border. Make sure that no part of the lawn or a grass path is narrower than the cutting width of your mower.

Plan to lay seep-hose among the plants before a border is finished, and then to hide it under a thick mulch. This will provide a simple, built-in watering system that only requires turning on at the faucet, and that reduces water loss through evaporation as water is retained by the mulch. A layer of mulch at least 2³/₄–4in (7–10cm) deep will also help to control weeds by stopping daylight from reaching the weed seeds, thereby preventing them from germinating. If a trellis is attached to a wall or fence, it can be hinged to allow it to swing free when the wall or fence needs painting or repairs.

ABOVE *Installing a mowing strip around the edge of the lawn will help reduce garden maintenance, as well as making grass cutting much easier and quicker.*

BELOW RIGHT *Using a range of plants with varied shapes and forms is not only pleasing to the eye, but also provides interest, which is of value for every season of the year.*

BELOW *A layer of mulch is useful for disguising a simple seep-hose irrigation system in borders.*

Design principles

When designing a garden, or part of a garden, it is important to keep the following points regarding scale, structure, and color in mind. The elements within a garden must all fit together, with no single item dominating the rest and distracting from the overall purpose and harmony of the garden.

SCALE, UNITY, AND PROPORTION The components of any design (plants, landscaping, and structures) should be in keeping with one another in terms of height, width, and length, so that they fit together visually. All the materials used should be in context with the site and its surroundings.

It can be difficult to envisage the final results of the design in the early stages, as there is a delay between planting young plants and their becoming established and large enough to be in scale with the rest of the garden. One solution is to plant a few big specimen plants among the smaller ones. Try to avoid the temptation to use too many different plants, which can make the garden look unbalanced and piecemeal.

Establish unity by selecting a range of similar plants, such as shade-loving or woodland plants, to create an atmosphere within the garden, or by using a path or lawn to flow through and link the different elements of a garden together. Balance can be maintained by making sure that every planted or structural area has an equal open area of grass or gravel. Decking can create unity if it is used in context, but it can also become dominant if it covers too large an area, or if the planking used is too wide.

ABOVE *A layer of morning frost adds a new dimension to plants trained as topiary. These plants offer winter protection for small birds.*

BELOW LEFT *Selecting plants with varied leaf shapes and textures for mixed borders can be a useful way of making a garden interesting even when there is a lack of flowers.*

BELOW *Hard materials, such as pots or gravel, can be used to complement plants. This urn is a focal point as well as a useful container.*

STRUCTURE AND COLOR A balanced sense of structure in the garden may require the repetition of certain basic shapes (circles or curves) or a theme, such as grass, decking, or paving. Establish a dominant style, either formal and geometric or informal and curvaceous—this may be determined by the setting of the garden and any surrounding buildings. Once chosen, the theme should be used throughout the design.

Use color to develop a theme or perception within the garden. Warm colors create a sense of warmth in a chilly, north-facing area and will foreshorten distances, giving a feeling of nearness. Cool colors make the distance recede and the garden seem longer than it actually is, as well as taking the heat out of a south-facing patio.

Gardening fashion influences color schemes. If you like a particular trend, use water-based paints for your garden furniture and short-lived plants, such as annuals, for your color scheme as these can be changed when the fashion changes. Having to replace trees, shrubs, and garden structures to follow the whims of fashion can be expensive in terms of both money and time.

Do not be put off by the prospect of trying to make all the elements of a design fit into place in the garden, because this is actually an easy task once you start to sketch out the main features on a piece of paper.

ABOVE *To gain the most impact from plants with colored stems, position them in front of a dark background, such as these conifers.*

BELOW *Shapely conifers with a light covering of snow create ghostly shapes when lit by a weak winter sun.*

Layout and measuring

In order to begin planning in earnest, the garden has to be measured to ascertain its size and total area, and the measurements recorded. You may also like to knock in marker pegs at regular intervals (for example every 3¼yd [3m]) to give an easy visual reference. Measuring is often easier if two people are involved—although moving the measuring tape is not difficult, it can be accomplished with greater ease when there is a person at each end.

ACCURATE MEASURING Before planning the layout of the new area, the boundaries must be measured and recorded so that they can be laid out on paper. Also note any dramatic changes in level, especially if you need to allow for leveling or steps. Note the position of any existing structures and features that are to remain. This planning is important for any garden, but particularly those where the development of individual areas may take several years. It will act as a point of reference in the future if more work is undertaken and will help to identify plants if their labels are lost.

Straightforward measuring in regular shapes, such as circles, squares, rectangles, and triangles, or from one point to another, is relatively easy, but what do you do if your garden is an irregular shape (as many gardens are)?

BELOW *When planning a garden, try to imagine just how large the plants will become when they mature. Allow new plants plenty of room to prevent future crowding and excessive competition.*

This is not as difficult a task as you might think, and the solution usually lies in dividing the area into smaller, more manageable segments, and then measuring each one individually.

SETTING OUT While the measuring is being done, use markers to indicate the position of certain features within the garden. If only one section of the garden is to be changed, that can be marked out with pegs. Wooden pegs are the easiest to use, with their ends painted a bright color so that they are easily spotted. These pegs can be knocked in to indicate the dimensions of features such as a patio or the line of a path, or to mark levels. Use different-colored pegs to indicate various features so that each can be separately identified, although there is a danger of the site resembling a large dartboard with lots of colored spikes embedded into it. Mark straight lines or boundaries with string, preferably brightly colored to help avoid tripping over it every few steps. Remember that your first plan is only a guide and will probably need some adjustment when the ideas are transferred from paper onto the ground, so be prepared to be flexible.

USING A SIMPLE SKETCH PLAN Place your ideas on paper to see what will fit where and to help keep the individual elements in the garden in perspective. Keep the plan simple—there is no real need for anything other than basic shapes and symbols, provided they are accurately positioned in relation to where they fit into the garden design.

TOP AND ABOVE *When measuring in the garden, always mark out a right angle at some point to help you get straight lines and accurate measurements. Always double-check at regular intervals.*

RIGHT *Draw a sketch plan of your garden to get an idea of its size and scale. Mark existing features onto the plan before adding any new ones.*

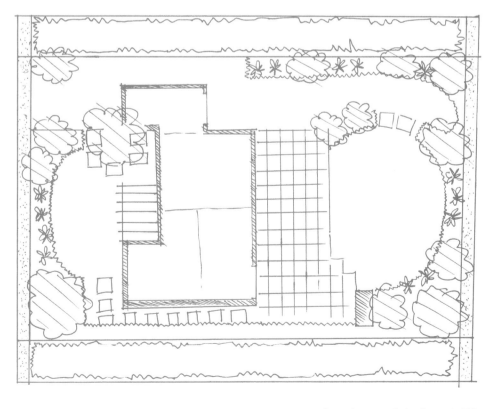

Leveling and earth moving

Leveling can be as simple or as complicated as you want to make it. For large areas, a sight level and tripod can be used, but for most gardens, a 1⅛yd (1m) carpenter's level, a long piece of timber with straight edges, wooden pegs, and a length of string are more than adequate. Winter is the best time to see where water collects and to plan drainage systems, and providing the ground is not frozen or waterlogged, it is also a good time to do the work, because many plants that need moving will be dormant (or almost so).

SETTING LEVELS   The easiest way to establish the level of a proposed area is to knock in a wooden peg at the correct level at a set point, such as near the wall of a house or a path that is to be kept in the new design. Use this as the main reference (datum) point, and use a carpenter's level to take readings from this point out into the garden. Rather than use too many pegs, a long (at least 2¼yd [2m]) wooden board with straight edges can be used to measure longer distances. Follow the natural lay of the land, aiming to modify existing levels rather than change the site, as this may undermine nearby foundations and can disrupt the natural drainage of the area.

On steeply sloping sites, longer wooden pegs will be needed to take a level reading when working down the slope. Use taut string from peg to peg to help indicate clearly the change in levels over the uneven ground. This can be very helpful when trying to gauge how much soil is to be moved from the upper to the lower sections of the garden.

ABOVE   *Strip off the turf before carrying out any major excavation work or releveling. The turf can be reused or stacked to rot down as garden compost.*

BELOW   *For existing lawns, strip off the turf before leveling the soil beneath. Good-quality turf can always be saved and reused. Cut-and-fill is a method of removing soil from the bumps to fill in the hollows and to level a site. Remove the topsoil first and replace it on the releveled site.*

ESTABLISHING THE DESIRED LEVEL

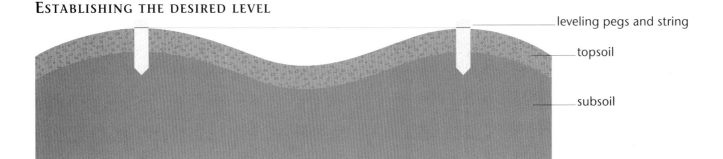

leveling pegs and string

topsoil

subsoil

THE LEVELED SOIL

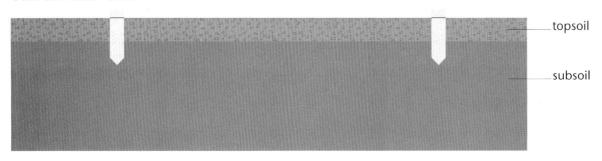

topsoil

subsoil

EARTH MOVING Gentle or undulating slopes can be leveled using a technique called "cut-and-fill," where the soil is scraped from the high points and used to fill the low points to achieve a reasonably level site. If the slope is steep, cut-and-fill will be impractical; instead, the garden can be divided up into sections and split levels or terraces created to tackle the slope gradually, giving the scope for a series of separate gardens.

If large quantities of soil are to be moved, strip off the topsoil (the top 8–10in [20–25cm]) and stack it on one side. Topsoil is the best soil for plant growth, so it should not be wasted. Level out the subsoil and firm it before replacing the topsoil. It is particularly important not to stack the topsoil more than about 16–18in (40–45cm) deep or the lower levels will lose their fertility due to a lack of oxygen, causing worms and beneficial bacteria to die. Also, if the topsoil is compacted when it is stacked, the air will be pressed out of it, leading to the same results. Few garden features or structures must have an absolutely level site, and patios and paths do benefit from a slight slope (or "fall") to allow for the drainage of surface water.

DRAINAGE During the process of earth moving, it is advisable to examine the soil to find out how quickly or slowly it drains by digging sight holes every 117sq yd (100sq m). These should be one to two spades wide and up to two spades deep to determine where the water table is (by how much water collects in the hole).

This is important if levels are going to be changed considerably, or if hard surfaces, such as paved patios, are going to be installed. It may be necessary to make a simple drainage system and to build a dry well to improve soil drainage. This is a large hole, dug at the lowest point in the garden and filled with rubble so that water is collected in it to drain away gradually.

What to keep and what to remove

Whenever a new design is being planned for a garden, there is always a great temptation to rip everything out, clear the site, and start again with a clean slate. Tempting though it is, this approach is wasteful in terms of plants, resources, time, and money, and unless radical changes are absolutely necessary, it is best avoided.

TAKING STOCK   It is amazing how many of the existing features can be moved around and transformed. Plants that did not look right in one corner could work well if moved across the garden. Where the garden is already established, it makes sense to look closely at the existing plants and features within it to see what is worth keeping. If possible, wait and watch for a complete year in order to see what happens in the garden during each season. This is time-consuming, especially if you are in a hurry to make your own mark on the place, but it will be worthwhile in the long run. In the meantime, buy plant labels and a marker pen to identify and tag those plants that are worth keeping. At this stage, plant names do not matter as much as recording the flower color and flowering time, which can help with

ABOVE   *By retaining some of the existing garden features, it is possible to give the new garden a feeling of maturity.*

BELOW   *Keeping a few, selected older plants will provide some shelter and protection for new introductions planted nearby.*

planning and arranging the plants later when changes are made. Decide on what your priorities and preferences are, and divide the plants and features into "need to keep," "nice to keep," and "got to go." Some items in the "nice to keep" category may include those that can be improved by remodeling or changing, such as a patio with a worn surface that could be used as the foundation for an attractive new wooden deck, or the surface removed and the foundation reused for new paving. Any structure that is to be dismantled or demolished can always be recycled—old bricks and paving can be used for building new paths or foundations. Discarded timber makes useful shuttering for concreting pathways or the base for a shed or greenhouse, and small pieces will make wooden pegs for marking out and setting levels.

ABOVE *Salvaging and recycling building materials can be both productive and cost-effective. Here a garden path is made to look old by using recycled bricks.*

WHAT CAN BE SAVED? By resiting some of the existing plants, you can create a framework that will help make the new garden look established more quickly. This approach is also cost-effective, as large, mature plants are expensive. It is even feasible to use these older plants as short-term "fillers" to protect the newly introduced plants. As the new plants become established, the older plants can be removed as necessary—this may be up to five years after the garden has been remodeled, but the shelter they provide will often help the new plants to establish more quickly.

Plants that are too big to transplant, or too old to be worth keeping, can be recycled by propagating them (taking cuttings or layering them) to give smaller, more vigorous versions of the original, or by shredding them into compost. Plants such as herbaceous perennials can be divided to produce numerous young plants, and the old core discarded. Propagating your own plants also makes your budget stretch further to fill the new garden.

LEFT *Logs and other timber can be saved and reused, making ideal edges for a border or natural-looking woodland steps in a garden that is on a split level.*

garden styles

As you start to consider a new design for your garden, have a good look around at other gardens in the area and at large gardens that are open to the public. Local conditions will dictate the range of plants you will be able to grow successfully, but the style in which you plant them will be entirely your own. The wider the range of options you view before starting your own project, the more likely it is that you will produce a garden you are pleased with.

ABOVE *The partially hidden stone lantern and tightly clipped topiary add a peaceful, almost Japanese, atmosphere to this area of the garden.*

If you decide to pursue a definite theme, such as a Japanese garden, then it is important to stick to it. The effect will be ruined if you succumb to an impulse buy at the nursery; for the keen gardener, this can require a massive amount of willpower. In this respect, a cottage garden is one of the easiest styles to choose because it is meant to be a mixture of plants, both ornamental and fruit and vegetables.

The size of your garden may have little bearing on the style chosen, but if it is small, you will probably have to scale down the elements of the design to fit in. Ponds can be designed in any shape or size, from the sweeping and dramatic to the tiny and delicate. Most good nurseries and garden centers will have a range of plants to suit any situation, from small alpines to large specimen shrubs and trees.

Within the design, there will be scope for using different surfaces, and a little variation can often enhance a design. Pockets left among paving can be filled with pebbles or cobbles (either loose or fixed), wood can be laid across a path at intervals, and paths and patios can be edged with a "soldier"

ABOVE *A sheltered sunny spot, with a seating area close by, is an ideal location for positioning fragrant winter plants in a garden.*

LEFT *The bold, symmetrical shapes and firm lines of a formal garden sprinkled with frost are seen emerging through the winter mists in early morning.*

course of bricks in a matching or contrasting color. Safety considerations mean that not every surface is suitable for every area, however. Loose gravel in a seating area may make the furniture unstable, for instance, so make sure you take these factors into account in the initial design.

The hard landscaping gives the garden a structure, but so do certain plants, and this fact becomes particularly important during the winter. Evergreens will blend into the background in summer when there are other, more colorful plants around, but in winter, when these ephemeral show-offs have died down, the shape, texture, and color of the evergreen will be a focal point in the grayness. This is even more obvious if the evergreen has a definite shape, such as a clipped topiary box (*Buxus*) or holly (*Ilex*). Likewise, a well-placed ornament will draw the eye, whether it is a statue, a Japanese lantern, or a decorative bamboo fence.

Scent in the garden is not something usually associated with winter, as we spend so little time outdoors. It comes as a pleasant surprise to open a window on a mild day to find a sweet scent drifting on the breeze. There are many plants that flower in winter and have the most delicious scent. If planted near windows, doors, and pathways, they are ideally placed to give the maximum pleasure.

winter
HARVEST

With only a few exceptions, such as artichokes and asparagus, vegetables tend to be relatively short-term crops because most are harvested before they reach maturity. In order to achieve this rapid growth, the ideal site for vegetables is one that is warm, with plenty of light and good air circulation, although sheltered from strong winds. Airflow is particularly important, to help reduce incidence of pests and diseases, which are always worse in still air conditions.

To achieve optimum growth, a gently sloping, south-facing site is ideal for vegetables growing outdoors in winter. Working can be difficult on very steep slopes, so the solution is to plant across the slope, rather than down it. This is easier on the gardener and also reduces the risk of soil erosion in periods of heavy rain, as the soil is less likely to be washed away down the slope.

If space is limited, a bed system can be used for growing vegetables. This is a multi-row system, with several rows of plants close together in beds. The beds are divided by pathways, allowing more plants to be grown per square yard or meter. When used across a sloping site, the lower side of the bed can be raised in order to create a terrace effect, which makes the slope more manageable and usually produces better vegetables.

There are a number of hardy vegetables that are favorites to grow at this time of year, such as Brussels sprouts, winter cabbage, winter cauliflower, leeks, winter spinach, kale, and parsnips—all seen as winter staples. There are also some more exotic-looking vegetables that are available fresh during the winter. Certain types of artichoke, Chinese broccoli, Chinese cabbage (pak choi), celeriac, red chicory, salsify, and scorzonera can all be grown in an average vegetable garden. In addition, there are those vegetables that have been harvested and stored for winter use, including beets, garlic, rutabagas, carrots, onions, turnips, and the humble potato. When listed in this way, the winter vegetable garden looks anything but limited.

RIGHT *Some types of cauliflower and cabbage will grow through the harsh winter weather before reaching maturity, in order to be ready for harvesting in late winter or early spring.*

planning and planting

For many gardeners, the challenge of growing vegetables is to try to produce a supply of food all year around, including the winter months, when the ones in the stores are at their most expensive. This can be achieved with careful planning to make the best use of the available space. Some room can also be set aside for those vegetables that grow through the winter but are harvested at other times of the year, such as fava beans, garlic, onions, celery, and asparagus.

BELOW *Raised beds are an ideal method of growing vegetables on heavy soils, and having permanent footpaths between the beds reduces soil compaction, especially during a wet growing season.*

BED SYSTEMS A bed system is one where several rows of plants are grown close together before being divided by a path. The distance between each row is the same as the distance between the plants (known as square plant arrangement), and although the pathways between the beds are slightly wider than those where plants are grown in rows, more plants are grown per square yard or meter because of the closer spacing within the multi-row bed.

The even plant arrangement, with equal space between the plants, means that the growth and shape of the vegetables is much more uniform, and the spacing can be adjusted to produce smaller vegetables if desired. Vegetables such as carrots, cauliflowers, and lettuces grown in this system will produce smaller mature plants for harvest (but often a higher yield per square yard or meter) than plants grown in rows because the competition between plants will determine the ultimate size.

Weed control is easier because the close spacing makes the competition too fierce for the weeds to establish, and as the vegetables grow large enough to cover the soil, the lack of light helps prevent weed seed germination. The soil structure benefits from the bed system and is kept in a better condition because there is less soil compaction overall when the pathways are farther apart. Ideally, the beds should be no more than 6ft (2m) wide, so that it is possible to reach the center of each bed from one of the pathways.

RAISED BEDS Building a frame for your vegetables, inside which the soil level can be raised above that of the surrounding soil, can have several benefits. On heavy soils, which may suffer from compaction when cultivated in wet conditions, this system of growing means that the roots are kept where the soil is drier, helping reduce root rot on plants that are growing slowly through the winter. The only usual solution to this problem is to work

Light, sandy soils, which may be lacking in humus, will benefit from a reduction in the level of cultivation that is usually necessary in a raised bed. Incorporating large amounts of organic matter in the soil will also help.

The sides of the bed need to be about 1ft (30cm) above soil level so that water can be taken up into the bed from the soil below by capillary action. If the beds are too high, the soil will dry out quickly, especially close to the sides, causing stress to those plants that are nearest.

DEEP BEDS The deep-bed method of growing involves double-digging the plot and incorporating large amounts of compost or manure to create a deep rooting zone for the plants. More dressings of organic matter are added at regular intervals, but there is no additional cultivation. The deep-bed system is more manageable if the bed is raised. This system is popular with organic gardeners, as it improves soil fertility and reduces the reliance on inorganic (chemical) fertilizers.

PLANT ARRANGEMENT Traditionally, vegetables have been grown close together in rows, with a wide space between the rows (a linear plant arrangement). The drawback to this method of growing is that the plants may become misshapen, due to irregular competition and having more light on two of the sides than on the other two. The alternative is to use a block or

ABOVE *Root vegetables, such as carrots, will need a deeply cultivated soil to allow their roots to penetrate and produce large crops.*

BELOW *Deep beds for growing vegetables are an ideal way to improve the rooting depth of plants, improve soil fertility, and preserve the soil structure.*

bed system, where the plants are an equal distance from one another (a square plant arrangement). Equal competition from all sides means that the plants will grow to a much more uniform shape. The beds should be about 5–6ft (1.5–2m) wide, so that the center of the bed can be reached from the pathway on each side. Several rows of plants are grown close together, with the distance between the rows being the same as the distance between the plants. Between the beds, the pathways are slightly wider than those on the row system, usually 2–2½ft (60–75cm) wide, but because of the closer plant spacing, more plants are grown per square yard or meter.

One drawback with this system is that the outer rows of the vegetable bed tend to produce plants that are slightly larger than those growing in the inner rows where the competition is greater. However, this can be compensated for by sowing or planting the outer rows at a slightly greater density than the inner rows. The practical application of changing plant arrangement and increasing plant density per square yard or meter is that it enables the gardener to use natural competition as a tool to determine the ultimate size of the vegetables.

ABOVE *Ruby chard is a hardy vegetable that is increasing in popularity. With its red leaf stalks and glossy leaves, it has an interesting ornamental value in the vegetable garden.*

CROP ROTATION   Crop rotation is a system used to move vegetable crops from one plot to another on a regular basis over a number of years. This reduces the chances of a buildup of pests and diseases within the soil that are specific to one plant or group of plants. Different plants remove nutrients from the soil at different rates, so rotating them also helps make the best use of the soil's natural resources. Some plants, such as peas and beans, which are able to harness atmospheric nitrogen and store it in their roots, actually add to the soil's reserves. Different crops need different types of cultivation and soil management, so rotation helps to protect the soil structure.

BELOW, LEFT TO RIGHT *Some vegetables, such as Savoy cabbage (left) are very hardy and are capable of withstanding extremely cold winters, but others will only survive if they get some protection, such as a covering of winter snow. Some, such as kale (center) and broccoli (right), need a period of cold to improve their flavor.*

Allocate each rotation group a plot of land and draw up a month-by-month cropping timetable. For example, crops of Brussels sprouts and leeks are cleared in early spring and can be followed by sowings of peas, carrots, lettuce, or salad onions. These may be from different crop groupings, which means that the rotation from one plot to another will be a gradual process, rather than a wholesale changeover on a preset date. This will keep the land fully occupied and provide continuity of crop management.

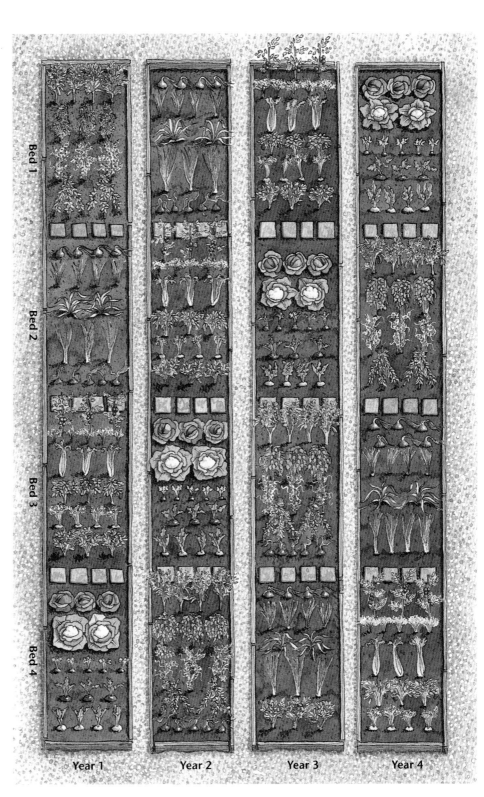

RIGHT *The suggested four-year crop rotation system illustrated here is an ideal method of growing vegetables to ensure that the most benefit is gained from the soil's natural fertility and to help reduce a buildup of pest and disease problems.*

Based on a four-year system, from left to right:

Year 1: *Bed 1 legumes: fava beans, french beans, peas, runner beans; Bed 2 onions: bulb onions, garlic, leeks, salad onions, shallots; Bed 3 roots and miscellaneous: carrots, celery, peppers, parsnips, potatoes, tomatoes; Bed 4 brassicas: cabbage, cauliflower, radish, rutabagas, turnip.*

Year 2: *Bed 1 onions: bulb onions, garlic, leeks, salad onions, shallots; Bed 2 roots and miscellaneous: carrots, celery, peppers, parsnips, potatoes, tomatoes; Bed 3 brassicas: cabbage, cauliflower, radish, rutabagas, turnip; Bed 4 legumes: fava beans, french beans, peas, runner beans.*

Year 3: *Bed 1 roots and miscellaneous: carrots, celery, peppers, parsnips, potatoes, tomatoes; Bed 2 brassicas: cabbage, cauliflower, radish, rutabagas, turnip; Bed 3 legumes: fava beans, french beans, peas, runner beans; Bed 4 onions: bulb onions, garlic, leeks, salad onions, shallots.*

Year 4: *Bed 1 brassicas: cabbage, cauliflower, radish, rutabagas, turnip; Bed 2 legumes: fava beans, french beans, peas, runner beans; Bed 3 onions: bulb onions, garlic, leeks, salad onions, shallots; Bed 4 roots and miscellaneous: carrots, celery, peppers, parsnips, potatoes, tomatoes.*

Bed 1

Bed 2

Bed 3

Bed 4

Year 1   Year 2   Year 3   Year 4

Winter crops

As soon as plants reach maturity, they begin to decline and will eventually rot, but before they reach that final stage they undergo a number of changes. This fact is important to keep in mind when growing a plant for food because the changes will affect its texture, nutritional content, and flavor. These changes are more critical than they would be in an ornamental plant. The main problem with growing vegetables in winter (root vegetables in particular) is that they have a high moisture content and are easily damaged, even if they are still in the soil. This damage is often caused by the speed at which the vegetable thaws out after a period of cold weather.

HARVESTING   The best way to prevent this deterioration is to harvest the produce when it has reached its peak of development and to eat it while it is still fresh and full of flavor. Unfortunately, this is not always possible. When and how the vegetables are harvested can have a great bearing on how well and how long they can be stored successfully. Rough handling during harvesting can damage the plant's outer tissues, which will have a number of detrimental effects on the produce. Damaged tissue will expend energy more quickly than healthy tissue, which speeds up the aging process and the deterioration of the vegetables. These areas are also much more susceptible to infection and rotting. For example, care must be taken when

ABOVE   *Vegetables such as turnips will survive outdoors in a mild winter, but storing is a wise precaution for colder areas.*

BELOW LEFT   *In very cold conditions, a loose covering of white horticultural fleece will act as an insulating blanket to protect growing plants from several degrees of frost without blocking the light.*

BELOW   *Brussels sprouts are very hardy and can be harvested continually from mid-fall through winter until spring.*

harvesting onions and potatoes, as both bruise very easily. Moving produce indoors as soon as possible after harvesting is particularly important to prevent them from drying out. One of the main causes of deterioration during storage is moisture loss from the plant tissue. Some vegetables, such as beets and carrots, dry out very quickly.

STORAGE   If the produce is not going to be used immediately, it is important to try to slow down these changes by careful storage in order to keep it in as perfect a condition as possible. In winter, the weather conditions mean that the vegetables are at risk of damage by freezing temperatures or cold, wet soil conditions, or a combination of the two. How long the vegetables can be stored will depend not only on the conditions within the storage area but also the vegetable type and cultivar.

FIELD STORAGE   Some root vegetables, such as carrots and parsnips, are very hardy and can be "field stored" in the ground until required, although this is only really feasible in raised beds or a free-draining soil. In poorly drained or wet soils these crops would suffer a high loss due to rotting.

ABOVE AND BELOW   *Although many herbs are readily available in dried form, some, such as basil and parsley, will remain fresh if they are grown as houseplants on a kitchen window sill.*

In extreme cold weather vegetables that are field stored need additional protection. Spread an 8in (20cm) layer of straw along the row of vegetables, followed by a layer of soil sprinkled over the straw to hold it in position and provide more protection; or drape fleece over the vegetables, with the edges buried in the soil to stop it from blowing away. It is important that the fleece is draped loosely over the vegetables, so that a layer of warm air can be trapped around them. However, these crops are prone to pest and disease attack throughout winter. Some leafy vegetables, such as Brussels sprouts, winter cabbage, and sprouting broccoli, are quite hardy and will survive outdoors in low temperatures. Many gardeners believe the flavor of Brussels sprouts improves after they have been frosted.

OUTDOOR STORAGE A traditional method of storing vegetables outdoors is to use a "clamp" or "pie" (see pages 46–7), but the site must be well drained. A cache of vegetables, such as carrots, potatoes, or turnips, is heaped into a mound and covered with straw and soil as a means of frost protection. The heap must be sited in a cool, shaded position, or the vegetables may start to sprout, which spoils their flavor and makes them susceptible to fungal rots.

ABOVE *Use a flat-tined fork to lift the crop. Allow potatoes to "sweat" for a while before storing them in a dry, frost-free shed.*

SOME WINTER VEGETABLES SUITABLE FOR FREEZING

Blanch before freezing

Beets

Brussels sprouts

Cabbages

Carrots

Cauliflowers

Kale

Kohl rabi

Parsnips

Potatoes

Spinach

Rutabagas

Turnips

Shred, purée, dice, or slice before freezing

Cauliflowers

Cabbages

Rutabagas

Turnips

DRY-STORED VEGETABLES Not all vegetables need to be kept in airtight containers—some need to dry slowly in a cool, dry place and others will keep for long periods in a similar atmosphere in a shed or cellar, in the case of brassicas with their outer leaves drying to protect the inner layer (or heart) from drying out. The storage area must be frost-free and as dark as possible. This is critical for potatoes because if they are stored in the light, poisonous alkaloids are produced in the tubers.

Autumn red cabbage and Dutch winter cabbage can be dry stored. Vegetables such as pumpkins, squashes, onions, and garlic will also store well in this way, but it is important to let the outer skin dry ("cure") in sunlight so that it hardens to protect the inner layers. Dry storage is also a useful method of storing a range of herbs used for seasoning.

FREEZING Many winter vegetables can be frozen (see left). This is better than leaving a mature crop to deteriorate in the field, as freezing suspends the development and aging of the produce and keeps it close to peak condition providing it is frozen rapidly. Only freeze produce that is in peak condition when harvested, and always prepare and clean it before storage.

LEFT *Red- and white-skinned onions and garlic will keep very well if they are hung in a dry, cool, frost-free room. It is important to allow onions to dry before they are stored. If they are not fully dry, they may start to rot from the top (the neck) and this can spread down into the main section of the bulb.*

RIGHT *Potatoes must be stored in a cool, dark, frost-free storage area or they will start to produce new shoots. Also, the skins of the potato tubers may turn green when exposed to daylight, and if these green-colored skins are eaten, they can cause stomach upsets or sickness.*

vegetable storage clamp

The traditional method for storing root vegetables is in a "clamp," or "pie." These are low mounds of vegetables, laid on a bed of loose straw to improve ventilation and prevent rotting. The top and sides of the mound are covered with a layer of loose straw for insulation and encased in a layer of soil or sand to hold the straw in place and provide extra protection.

These clamps can be made either outside on a well-drained site or under cover in a shed or outbuilding. Although the storage conditions are very similar to those in the ground, a clamp is often more convenient. It is easier to remove vegetables from the storage clamp in severe cold weather when the ground is frozen than it is to dig them out of the soil in the vegetable plot.

Unfortunately, the amount of waste, from rodents and rotting, can be high. For extra protection, the clamp may be formed against a wall or hedge, and if long-term storage is the objective, choose a north-facing site if possible, as this will receive much less direct sunlight in the winter months.

AUTHOR'S TIP:
Drainage system

Dig a trench around the base of the clamp to provide soil to cover the straw-clad clamp. The trench will also provide drainage at the base of the clamp, which, in turn, reduces the chances of rotting and makes it easier to see if vermin are starting to burrow into the clamp.

CLOCKWISE FROM TOP LEFT

Clear and level the area of ground where the vegetables are to be stored (it is important to select a site with a free-draining soil).

Spread out a layer of dry, loose straw to cover the area to a depth of about 8in (20cm).

Build up a mound of vegetables on the straw to form a cone shape to the required height (carrots should not be stacked more than 2½ft [75cm] high).

Once the mound of vegetables has reached the required height, cover the whole mound with a 6in (15cm) layer of dry straw.

Cover the mound with a layer of soil about 4in (10cm) deep. The soil is provided by digging a trench around the base of the clamp for drainage, and throwing the resulting soil up over the straw-covered mound.

Finally, firm the soil over the mound by patting it down with the back of a spade. This helps keep the straw dry and reduces the chances of rain washing the soil down from the top of the mound. Leave a small area of straw exposed at the top of the clamp, to act as a ventilator and allow any warm air to escape from the clamp, keeping the vegetables cooler.

TOOLS FOR THE JOB
1 garden fork
1 spade
1 wheelbarrow

MATERIALS
2 bales of straw
Quantity of root vegetables for storage
(potatoes, carrots, or other)

storage of root vegetables

Many root vegetables are stored in boxes over winter to protect them from frost, and for convenience, these boxes are often placed in sheds or basements. It is often much easier to collect vegetables stored in this way than it is to go outdoors in winter weather to collect field-stored vegetables, or even vegetables stored in a clamp (see pages 46–7).

Boxes or barrels of slightly moist sand are used to keep produce fresh and to extend its storage life. Ideally, these containers should be kept in a frost-free place to protect their contents as much as possible. Vegetables stored in this way must be handled carefully to reduce the risk of bruising, and any soil must be cleaned off the produce before it is stored. Soil left on the roots may contain fungal or bacterial spores, which can attack the produce and cause it to rot while it is in storage.

Never store any vegetables that are showing signs of rotting or severe damage. These "suspect" vegetables will be a source of primary infection, causing rotting among the healthy plants, and should be discarded straightaway. Use any lightly damaged vegetables as they will also rot quickly.

AUTHOR'S TIP:
Retaining moisture

Keep the sand moist at all times. If it dries out, it will draw the moisture out of the vegetables, causing them to desiccate and spoil. Plastic containers do not lose moisture as readily as wooden crates or boxes.

CLOCKWISE FROM TOP LEFT

Harvest the vegetables that are to be stored. Handling them carefully, brush off any loose soil. For vegetables such as beets, carrots, parsnips, and turnips, trim off leaves and stalks and remove any long, thin roots. Discard all vegetables that show signs of rot or damage. Wash the vegetables to remove any remaining soil and leave them until the water has drained away, but the surface of the vegetables is still moist.

Place a sturdy container, such as a barrel or box, in a frost-free site where the temperature is just above freezing. Cover the bottom of the container with a 4in (10cm) layer of damp sand. Remove any stones or gravel to avoid them damaging the vegetables.

Place a layer of vegetables onto the sand, with the root tips facing into the center of the container. Cover with a layer of sand and another layer of vegetables. Make sure that the vegetables are not touching one another, as this will help prevent the spread of fungal or bacterial rots. Place the largest vegetables at the bottom and the smallest at the top (the smallest are prone to drying out and should be used first).

Repeat this process until the container is filled to within 6in (15cm) of the upper rim. Place at least 2in (5cm) of sand between each layer of vegetables and the sides of the container.

Cover the topmost layer of vegetables with a 6in (15cm) layer of damp sand. Gently pack the sand down to remove as much air from it as possible, and lightly water it to form a surface crust or "seal" to reduce moisture loss. Check frequently to see if it is drying out. If it becomes too dry, gently moisten it with a fine spray from a watering can.

TOOLS FOR THE JOB
1 brush (for cleaning)
1 knife or pair of pruning shears
1 bucket
1 watering can or hose
1 wheelbarrow
1 spade or shovel

MATERIALS
1 or more containers, for example
a wooden box or plastic trash can
Quantity of washed sand
Quantity of root vegetables for storage
(the container should hold 50 percent
vegetables and 50 percent sand)

PROJECT 3

making a raised vegetable bed *Using raised beds, or a deep-bed system, for growing vegetables is an ideal way of maintaining a vegetable garden in a small area, or as a method of keeping the vegetable garden more clearly defined and easy to manage. Raised beds also encourage plants to root more deeply into the soil so that less watering is required.*

Growing plants close together in a bed system increases competition between the individual plants and is a means of producing slightly smaller vegetables, or "mini-vegetables," which are ideal for people living alone, or in couples (rather than a family). The high density of plants cuts down the amount of light reaching the soil's surface and so reduces the germination of weed seeds and the development of weed seedlings.

It is worth remembering that it is more important to practice crop rotations in these confined beds than in a larger area of a vegetable garden as the planting is so intensive, and a buildup of specific pests and diseases must be avoided. Due to the improved drainage, field storage of winter vegetables is much more successful in raised beds than with other growing methods.

AUTHOR'S TIP:
Improving fertility

The topsoil cleared from leveled areas can often be used to fill raised beds, or mixed with some new topsoil, incorporating plenty of bulky organic matter such as compost or well-rotted manure to encourage greater bacterial and worm activity. These bulky materials also retain more moisture, which reduces the need to water the plants as frequently in dry weather.

CLOCKWISE FROM TOP LEFT

Clear and level the area for the raised bed. Using bamboo sticks and a tape measure, mark out a rectangular area measuring about 6 x 6ft (2 x 2m).

Cut four 4 x 4in (10 x 10cm) pieces of timber to 12in (30cm) long to form the four corner posts of the raised bed, plus two extra pieces of timber to support the sides and give extra strength (especially if the sides of the bed are more than 5ft [1.5m] long). Knock in a post at each corner of the marked area.

Use lengths of 1 x 6in (2.5 x 15cm) nonresistant wood, such as redwood, black locust, cedar, or cypress, for the sides and ends of the bed. Put the lengths of wood in place and use a builder's square to check the right angles of the structure. Nail the wood to the corner posts to form a rectangular frame.

Add extra soil to the bed, mixing it with the existing soil to aid drainage and water movement.

Firm the soil well to reduce uneven settling later when the plants are in place.

A layer of organic mulch will improve the fertility of the soil. When planting vegetables in the new bed, place them slightly closer together than for growing plants in rows.

TOOLS FOR THE JOB
1 garden fork or rake
1 spade or shovel
1 claw hammer
1 wood saw
1 builder's square

MATERIALS
1 x 6ft (2m) long, 4 x 4in (10 x 10cm) lengths of timber for the corner posts

12 x 6ft (2 x 2m) long, 1 x 6in (2.5 x 15cm) wood treated with preservative (or your desired length) for the sides

12 x 12ft (2 x 2m) long 1 x 6in (2.5 x 15cm) wood treated with preservative (or your desired length) for the ends

50 x 4in (10cm) galvanized nails

vegetable directory

Work in the vegetable garden continues throughout the winter months, protecting the harvest from the winter weather in order to ensure a steady supply of vegetables during the coldest months of the year.

HARDY WINTER VEGETABLES THAT CAN SURVIVE OUTDOORS

VEGETABLE	DESCRIPTION	HARVESTING AND STORAGE
	Allium porrum (Leek) Leeks are grown for their white, fleshy leaf bases, which are tightly packed together to form a stemlike shank or "leg." If you opt for a hardy variety, they have a long cropping season from early fall, through the winter, and into late spring the following year.	Leeks are harvested by lifting them from the ground when they are required for use and are hardy enough to tolerate winter conditions if they are mulched to keep the soil from freezing. In cold weather mature leeks can stand for up to four months.
	Apium graveolens rapaceum (Celeriac) This vegetable, a close relative of celery, is grown for its celery-flavored swollen stem, which takes six months to develop. It can be used cooked or raw and is often the main ingredient in celery soup.	Once the root is 2in (5cm) or more in diameter, mulch the roots in fall to extend the harvest period. Harvest celeriac by digging up with a fork from early fall through until the following spring.
	Beta vulgaris cicla (Swiss chard) This close relative of beets is grown for its large, succulent glossy leaves, some up to 18in (45cm) long and 8in (20cm) wide. The best known form is ruby chard, which is easy to grow.	This hardy crop can be harvested through the winter, with some plants lasting almost a full year. It self-sows readily.
	Brassica oleracea botrytis (Cauliflower) Usually harvested while the immature flower head, or "curd," is developing, often producing curds up to 1ft (30cm) across.	Fall cauliflowers are ready for harvest from late summer until midwinter; winter cauliflowers are ready from late winter through until early spring. The covering leaves will start to open, showing the enclosed curd beneath. Remove the curd by cutting through the main stem with a sharp knife, taking a row of leaves as well, to protect the curd from becoming marked.
	Brassica oleracea capitata (Cabbage) Winter cabbage is hardy, particularly the Savoy type and should be planted in midsummer, ready for harvest from late fall through to mid-spring.	When the cabbage has developed a good, solid heart, it is ready for harvesting. Using a sharp knife, cut through the main stem to remove all of the heart and a few outer leaves, leaving the stem and oldest leaves in the soil. Store the cabbage in a dry, frost-free place, such as a basement or shed.
	Brassica oleracea gemmifera (Brussels sprouts) A hardy vegetable grown for its edible flower buds, which form small, tight sprouts on the main stem. Some of the older cultivars, such as 'Bedfordshire Giant', will grow up to 6ft (2m) tall and are ideal for small gardens where space is limited.	Harvesting can be any time from early fall through to mid-spring. Pull the sprouts downward so that they snap from the stem. Toward the end of the season, the tops of the plants can be snapped off and eaten like spring greens.
	Brassica oleracea italica (Broccoli) Sprouting broccoli is a very hardy winter vegetable. There are both white- and purple-flowered forms, with the purple one being the hardier.	Broccoli is usually harvested from late winter until late spring. Start by cutting the central spike first; the slightly smaller spikes can be cut later.

VEGETABLE	DESCRIPTION	HARVESTING AND STORAGE
	Brassica napobrassica (Rutabaga) This is one of the hardiest of all root crops and is grown for its creamy-white or yellow flesh and mild, sweet flavor. It can be identified by the leaf scars on top of the root.	Rutabagas are usually ready from early to mid-fall onward. They can be left outdoors through the winter, stored in boxes of damp sand or in a clamp.
	**Brassica oleracea sabellica** (Kale) The hardiest of winter vegetables, yielding tasty shoots and leaves. Capable of producing early growth in the spring and especially valued after a severe winter.	Harvest on a cut-and-come-again approach by snapping off the young leaves from all of the plants. This prevents any leaves maturing and becoming tough and stringy.
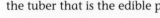	**Helianthus tuberosus** (Jerusalem artichoke) This is a vigorous, perennial plant that is very good for helping to clear rough ground. It is the tuber that is the edible part of the plant.	Tubers are ready for lifting from mid-fall onward and are dug up with a fork for immediate use or storage. In well-drained soils, the tubers can overwinter in the growing site.
	Pastinaca sativa (Parsnip) A valuable hardy, winter root vegetable with a very distinctive flavor. The roots are hardy enough to overwinter in the soil. They prefer a deep, stone-free, well-drained, fertile soil.	Roots are ready for lifting from mid-fall onward and are dug up with a fork for immediate use or storage.

WINTER VEGETABLES THAT NEED STORAGE AND PROTECTION

VEGETABLE	DESCRIPTION	HARVESTING AND STORAGE
	**Allium cepa** (Onion) Bulb onions are grown as annual plants. The brown- or yellow-skinned cultivars are the most popular. Onions have a long growing season, and for good skin color the bulbs need a period of bright sun before harvesting.	Lift the bulbs gently with a digging fork and allow them to dry naturally before they are taken into storage in a cool, dry place.
	Beta vulgaris (Beet) This is a useful vegetable with a swollen, edible root that can be globular or tapered. Beets can be used at just about any time of year, either fresh, stored, or pickled.	Beets are not fully hardy and should be lifted for storage by late fall. Dig up the roots with a garden fork and twist off the leaves before storing them in moist sand in a cool, dry, frost-free shed.
	**Allium sativum** (Garlic) This hardy vegetable with its strong characteristic flavor is far easier to grow than many gardeners realize. There are two distinctive forms, one white-skinned and the other purple.	Garlic bulbs should be lifted and dried as soon as the leaves start to turn yellow. The bulbs can be stored in cool, dry conditions for up to 10 months.
	Brassica rapa (Turnip) This winter vegetable has a large, swollen root with white flesh. Turnips can be available throughout the year, if a range of different cultivars is grown in succession.	Turnips are usually ready from early to mid-fall onward but must be lifted by Christmas and taken into storage in a cool, dry place. Store for up to four months.
	Solanum tuberosum (Potatoes) This versatile vegetable is grown for its tubers (which are actually modified stems) that contain protein, vitamin C, and dietary fiber.	To harvest potatoes, dig into the ridge of earth in which they are growing using a garden fork. Always start digging under the ridge of earth, to avoid stabbing any of the tubers. Potatoes must always be stored in a cool, dark, frost-free place, and some cultivars will keep until the following summer.

winter
FLOWERS

Plants that flower during winter provide an outstanding display in terms of both flowers and smell; indeed, many winter flowers are strongly and sweetly scented in order to attract the few pollinating insects that survive winter conditions. Some, such as the winter-flowering cherry (*Prunus* x *subhirtella*) Autumnalis' and winter jasmine (*Jasminum nudiflorum*), will bloom almost continuously from late fall until early spring if the conditions are right.

Most plant categories contain examples that will flower in winter, though in slightly different ways according to the weather. Of the shrubs, witch hazels (*Hamamelis* species and cultivars) tend to flower at about the same time each year, regardless of temperature. Other plants, such as bush honeysuckle (*Lonicera fragrantissima*), flower during the warmer days after a period of cold, but the flowers may be spoiled if the temperature falls back below freezing, and they will not produce more until the weather warms up again.

Bulbs have their part to play in the winter garden, with their delicate-looking flowers displaying an unbelievable hardiness even in quite extreme weather conditions. The capacity of bulb flowers to survive apparently hostile conditions means that it is possible to have snowdrops (*Galanthus* species) flowering continually from midwinter right through until late spring.

Some herbaceous perennials are closely associated with the winter garden. Many hellebores flower profusely in winter, with *Helleborus niger* blooming well enough to be dubbed the "Christmas rose." Winter-flowering climbers are represented by *Clematis napaulensis* in midwinter and *C. cirrhosa*, which will bloom almost constantly throughout the winter months.

The following are a selection of the best winter-flowering plants. The snowflake symbols indicate the minimum winter temperatures that the plants can withstand and are based on the United States Department of Agriculture zone system (see page 192 for temperature ranges).

RIGHT *Some hardy bulbs, such as this winter aconite (*Eranthis hyemalis*), seem determined to produce flowers in total defiance of the cold, hostile winter weather.*

winter-flowering guide

While winter may seem a rather bare time of year, there are many plants that provide winter interest. This interest may be in the guise of colored stems and bark, colorful foliage, flowers or fruits, or interesting shapes.

TYPE	NAME	FEATURE	DURATION	ZONE
ANNUALS	BELLIS PERENNIS + CULTIVARS	FLOWERS	FEB–APR	✳✳✳✳
	ERYSIMUM CHEIRI + CULTIVARS	FLOWERS	FEB–MAY	✳✳✳✳✳✳✳
	MYOSOTIS SYLVATICA + CULTIVARS	FLOWERS	FEB–APR	✳✳✳✳✳
	VIOLA CULTIVARS	FLOWERS	OCT–APR	✳✳✳✳✳✳
BULBS	ANEMONE BLANDA + CULTIVARS	FLOWERS	JAN–FEB	✳✳✳✳✳
	CROCUS BIFLORUS	FLOWERS	JAN–APR	✳✳✳✳
	CROCUS CHRYSANTHUS + CULTIVARS	FLOWERS	JAN–APR	✳✳✳✳
	CYCLAMEN COUM	FLOWERS	FEB–MAR	✳✳✳✳
	CYCLAMEN HEDERIFOLIUM	FLOWERS	OCT–NOV	✳✳✳✳✳
	ERANTHIS HYEMALIS	FLOWERS	JAN–MAR	✳✳✳✳✳
	GALANTHUS SPECIES + CULTIVARS	FLOWERS	FEB–MAY	✳✳✳✳ (✳✳)
	NARCISSUS JONQUILLA	FLOWERS	FEB–APR	✳✳✳✳
	SCILLA SIBIRICA	FLOWERS	FEB–MAR	✳✳✳✳✳
HERBACEOUS PERENNIALS	BERGENIA CORDIFOLIA	FLOWERS/LEAVES	FEB–APR	✳✳✳
	BERGENIA CRASSIFOLIA	FLOWERS/LEAVES	FEB–APR	✳✳✳
	BERGENIA PURPURASCENS	FLOWERS/LEAVES	FEB–APR	✳✳✳✳
	BRASSICA OLERACEA	LEAVES	OCT–APR	✳✳✳✳✳✳✳
	HELLEBORUS FOETIDUS	FLOWERS	DEC–FEB	✳✳✳✳✳✳
	HELLEBORUS NIGER	FLOWERS	NOV–FEB	✳✳✳
	HELLEBORUS ORIENTALIS	FLOWERS	FEB–MAR	✳✳✳✳✳✳
CLIMBERS	CLEMATIS ARMANDII + CULTIVARS	FLOWERS	MAR–APR	✳✳✳✳✳✳
	CLEMATIS CIRRHOSA VAR. BALEARICA	FLOWERS	NOV–MAR	✳✳✳✳✳✳
	CLEMATIS NAPAULENSIS	FLOWERS	DEC–JAN	✳✳✳✳✳✳✳
	HEDERA COLCHICA + CULTIVARS	LEAVES	OCT–APR	✳✳✳✳✳✳
	HEDERA HELIX + CULTIVARS	LEAVES	OCT–APR	✳✳✳✳✳✳
	JASMINUM NUDIFLORUM	FLOWERS	NOV–MAR	✳✳✳✳✳✳
SHRUBS	ABELIOPHYLLUM DISTICHUM	FLOWERS	FEB–MAR	✳✳✳✳✳
	AUCUBA JAPONICA + CULTIVARS	LEAVES	OCT–APR	✳✳✳✳✳✳✳
	BERBERIS DICTYOPHYLLA	STEMS	OCT–APR	✳✳✳✳✳✳
	CORNUS ALBA + CULTIVARS	STEMS	OCT–APR	✳✳✳
	CORNUS SANGUINEA 'WINTER BEAUTY'	STEMS	OCT–APR	✳✳✳✳✳
	CORNUS STOLONIFERA 'FLAVIRAMEA'	STEMS	OCT–APR	✳✳
	ERICA X DARLEYENSIS	FLOWERS/LEAVES	DEC–MAR	✳✳✳✳✳✳
	ERICA ERIGENA + CULTIVARS	FLOWERS/LEAVES	NOV–MAR	✳✳✳✳✳✳✳

TYPE	NAME	FEATURE	DURATION	ZONE
SHRUBS (continued)	FORSYTHIA GIRALDIANA	FLOWERS	FEB–MAR	❄❄❄❄❄
	LONICERA FRAGRANTISSIMA	FLOWERS	NOV–MAR	❄❄❄❄❄
	LONICERA STANDISHII	FLOWERS	NOV–MAR	❄❄❄❄❄❄
	ROSA RUGOSA + CULTIVARS	FRUITS	OCT–APR	❄❄
	RUBUS COCKBURNIANUS + CULTIVARS	STEMS	OCT–APR	❄❄❄❄❄
	SALIX ALBA SUBSP. VITELLINA	STEMS	OCT–APR	❄❄
	SALIX ALBA SUBSP. VITELLINA 'BRITZENSIS'	STEMS	OCT–APR	❄❄
	SALIX SACHALINENSIS 'SEKKA'	STEMS/FORM	OCT–APR	❄❄❄❄❄
	SARCOCOCCA SPECIES + CULTIVARS	FLOWERS	DEC–FEB	❄❄❄❄❄❄ (❄❄❄)
	SKIMMIA JAPONICA + CULTIVARS	FLOWERS/FRUIT	FEB–APR	❄❄❄❄❄❄
	SYMPHORICARPUS SPECIES + CULTIVARS	FRUITS	OCT–APR	❄❄ (❄❄❄❄)
	VIBURNUM X BODNANTENSE + CULTIVARS	FLOWERS	NOV–FEB	❄❄❄❄❄❄
	VIBURNUM FARRERI	FLOWERS	NOV–FEB	❄❄❄❄❄
	VIBURNUM FOETENS	FLOWERS	DEC–FEB	❄❄❄❄❄
	VIBURNUM TINUS + CULTIVARS	FLOWERS	NOV–MAR	❄❄❄❄❄❄
LARGE SHRUBS or SMALL TREES	COTONEASTER SPECIES + CULTIVARS	FRUITS	OCT–APR	❄❄❄❄❄ (❄❄)
	HAMAMELIS X INTERMEDIA + CULTIVARS	FLOWERS	DEC–MAR	❄❄❄❄❄
	HAMAMELIS JAPONICA + CULTIVARS	FLOWERS	DEC–MAR	❄❄❄❄❄
	HAMAMELIS MOLLIS + CULTIVARS	FLOWERS	NOV–JAN	❄❄❄❄❄
	ILEX SPECIES + CULTIVARS	LEAVES/FRUIT	OCT–APR	❄❄❄❄❄❄
TREES	ACER DAVIDII + VARIETIES + CULTIVARS	BARK	OCT–APR	❄❄❄❄❄
	ACER GRISEUM	BARK	OCT–APR	❄❄❄❄❄
	ACER PENSYLVANICUM	BARK	OCT–APR	❄❄❄
	ARBUTUS SPECIES + CULTIVARS	FLOWERS/FRUIT	OCT–JAN	❄❄❄❄❄❄
	BETULA ALBOSINENSIS + VARIETIES	BARK	OCT–APR	❄❄❄❄❄❄
	BETULA PAPYRIFERA	BARK	OCT–APR	❄❄
	BETULA UTILIS + VARIETIES + CULTIVARS	BARK	OCT–APR	❄❄❄❄❄❄
	CORNUS MAS	FLOWERS	JAN–FEB	❄❄❄❄❄
	PARROTIA PERSICA	FLOWERS	DEC–FEB	❄❄❄❄❄
	PRUNUS MAACKII	STEMS	OCT–APR	❄❄
	PRUNUS X SUBHIRTELLA + CULTIVARS	FLOWERS	NOV–MAR	❄❄❄❄❄
	SALIX 'ERYTHROFLEXUOSA'	STEMS/FORM	OCT–APR	❄❄❄❄❄
	SORBUS HUPEHENSIS	FRUITS	OCT–APR	❄❄❄❄❄❄
	STACHYURUS PRAECOX	FLOWERS	NOV–MAR	❄❄❄❄❄❄

annuals

Some of the most colorful plants we grow in our gardens are annuals grown from seed. However, the range of annuals suitable for use in a winter garden is limited, as many of the plants, by their very nature, are not fully hardy and stand little chance of surviving a winter outdoors without protection. Even with protection, most plants within this group, although considered hardy annuals, would be unable to flower, and so provide very little color or interest over the winter period. In reality, many of the plants considered to be "winter annuals" are in fact biennials.

Biennials produce leaves and shoots in their first year and flower the following year, often using up their stockpiled food reserves in the process. They offer good value and are useful for providing quick, bright colors because they require limited space and give a rapid return in terms of the short growing period prior to flowering. Wallflowers (*Erysimum cheiri*) are a prime example of this. Although biennials do not have a long life, many make up for this by self-seeding. Unless the plants (or flower heads) are removed soon after flowering, the seeds they cast onto the soil will emerge as new plants in the same area the following year. It is worth bearing in mind that although the original plants are hybrids, the seedlings they produce will not be true to type and will vary slightly—but they are no less colorful. Some plants, such as pansies, now have summer- and winter-flowering strains available, making it possible to have them in flower all year round.

If a garden has not been planned to have winter color, it is possible to use these plants as "fillers," positioned between plants that flower at other times of the year but that can be rather drab in the winter months. The range of plants may be small, but those used are fairly well known, as they are regularly used in formal beds, as edgings to mixed borders, as groups of plants dotted into shrub borders, or as seasonal plantings in containers. For gardening enthusiasts who have little space, or are limited to window box gardening, these short-term, winter-flowering plants are a must, needing little care and attention, but capable of flowering for long periods in mild winters or flowering through every mild period during harder winters. These plants can also be used with bulbs, to provide a display from midwinter into spring, with the bulbs emerging to liven it up just as it starts to look tired.

RIGHT Erysimum cheiri *is hardy enough to survive winter outdoors and produce a display of color in late winter and early spring.*

RIGHT, FAR RIGHT, BELOW RIGHT, AND BOTTOM *Among the most popular winter- and spring-flowering plants are pansies and violas. They range from the smaller-flowered species, which produce a discreet but prolific display of flowers, to the larger-flowered hybrids, which are the result of a number of years of plant breeding and selection. These can range from single-colored, named selections through to seedling populations, which tend to have variable, mixed flower colors but uniform growth and height patterns.*

Bellis perennis

The English daisy is a short-lived perennial, which is usually grown as a biennial or a winter annual. This plant is valued for its small, pomponlike flowers, which have one or more rows of outer petals, in shades of pink, red, and pure white, usually with a golden center of smaller florets, produced from late winter until early summer. The Tasso Series has large flower heads of needlelike petals; the Habanera Series produces large flowers; and the Roggli Series bears semidouble blooms. These hardy, stocky plants have a "rosette" habit, reach up to 4in (10cm) in height and will form a spreading clump about 6–8in (15–20cm) across. They have glossy to mid-green, spoon-shaped leaves, often covered in a layer of short, fine hairs. ❋ ❋ ❋ ❋

Propagation is usually from seed, although plants can be divided and replanted immediately after flowering.

Erysimum cheiri

This hardy plant used to have the botanical name *Cheiranthus cheiri*, and although the Latin name has changed, the common name of wallflower remains. This is a short-lived perennial, which is usually grown as a biennial. A late winter- and spring-flowering plant, it is much valued for its dense clusters of fragrant, brightly colored blooms, ranging from white through yellows, oranges, and pinks to deep blackish red, carried on the tips of the shoots. There are a number of outstanding color mixtures: 'Bedding Mixed' has a range of bold colors, 'Monarch Fair Lady' has a wide variety of pastel colors, or for a single color, 'Ruby Gem' has fragrant, violet-ruby flowers. The narrow, straplike leaves are a mid- to deep green and are arranged close together on stocky pale green stems reaching up to 2ft (60cm) in height. Side shoots emerge from the bottom half of the plant to produce the second flush of flowers. ❋ ❋ ❋ ❋ ❋ ❋ ❋

Propagation is by seed sown in late spring, although there are some named cultivars that can be propagated by semi-ripe cuttings taken in mid- to late summer.

Myosotis sylvatica

Commonly known as the forget-me-not, this plant has tiny, fragrant, flat flowers borne on dense spikes. They open from late winter until early summer, with colors ranging from purple to blue or white, often with a distinctive yellow eye. The broadly spear-shaped leaves are hairy and mid-green in color and carried on hairy, reddish green stems to form a dense bushy plant about 1ft (30cm) high and spreading to form a clump 10ft (25cm) across. There are now many garden hybrids, including 'Blue Ball', which makes a compact ball-shaped plant with deep blue flowers, or colored-flower variants such as 'Carmine King', which has an erect habit with deep rose-carmine flowers, and 'Alba', which has white flowers with a bright yellow eye in the center. These tough plants are quite hardy, preferring a well-drained soil and a partially shaded site. ❋ ❋ ❋ ❋ ❋ ❋ ❋

Sow the seeds in spring, then divide when dormant. Propagate on a regular basis. Prone to damage by snails or slugs.

Viola

The pansy is one of the most popular garden plants for winter bedding, patio containers, hanging baskets, and window boxes. They are fairly low-growing plants, reaching up to 6–8in (15–20cm) high, and about 1ft (30cm) across. The flowers range in size from 1in (2.5cm) to 2¾in (7.5cm) across, with a range of colors varying from golden yellow, through to reds, whites, and deep violets, often bicolored. The narrow, oval-shaped leaves have toothed edges, are a glossy mid-green in color, and are carried on lax, spreading stems. The winter-flowering strains can be bought as mixed colors, such as 'Roggli Giant Strain', but named single-color varieties are also available; 'Irish Molly' is a copper yellow, 'Jolly Joker' orange and purple, and 'Primrose Dame' is primrose yellow. ❋ ❋ ❋ ❋ ❋ ❋

These hardy, resilient plants are propagated from seed, and will grow well in a wide range of conditions.

ABOVE LEFT 'Universal' pansies are grown for their large, bold-colored flowers and will often grow for a second season if left undisturbed.

TOP Erysimum cheiri 'Golden Bedder' is a hardy, reliable performer with a long flowering season.

ABOVE This delicate-looking English daisy (Bellis perennis) is actually extremely hardy.

LEFT Forget-me-not (Myosotis sylvatica) is a reliable early spring performer, often showing its blue, pink, or white flowers very early in the year.

annuals ✳ 61

bulbs

One of the most popular groups of plants to grow in the garden are bulbs, although the term "bulb" tends to cover all plants with a swollen storage organ, including true bulbs, corms, tubers, and rhizomes. Bulbs originate from a variety of areas, including the Himalayas, Afghanistan, Turkey and the Mediterranean, South Africa, and California. Many are among the hardiest and most resilient plants grown in our gardens, and few gardening pleasures equal that of seeing a snowdrop or crocus poke a bloom through the earth in winter, when so many other plants are dormant.

Bulbs are commonly associated with late winter and spring, but the range now available means that it is possible to have colorful bulb flowers in every season of the year. So, while winter is a time for appreciating those bulbs that are flowering, it is also the season for planting bulbs to bloom during spring, summer, and fall.

Bulbs require a regular supply of water when growing and flowering; however, few will tolerate wet soil and most prefer a sunny, well-drained position. Exceptions include the hardy cyclamen (*Cyclamen coum*), which will grow in a shady position, and winter aconite (*Eranthis hyemalis*) and snowdrop (*Galanthus nivalis*), which tolerate moist soils and shade from trees above.

Naturalizing bulbs by growing them through grass will also help keep them drier through the winter months, as the slow-growing grass draws water from the soil. This is the best option for bulbs that can compete with grass or that do not like to be disturbed. For best effect, they should be planted thickly to form carpets of flowers. It is important to leave foliage uncut for at least six weeks after flowering, as mowing too soon will weaken the bulb, reduce flowering, and may eventually kill the bulb.

For smaller or less vigorous bulbs, which can be naturalized but do not compete well with grass, woodland and shrub borders are a good alternative to grass. As the soil is usually uncultivated in these areas, apart from weed control, this means that the bulbs are left undisturbed to establish and colonize. Varieties can be chosen to suit the different conditions provided by the canopy of plants, ranging from dappled shade to full sun. If the canopy becomes too dense once the leaves have opened fully, then choose bulbs that flower early in the year, before the leaves unfurl.

RIGHT *Large groups (or drifts) of flowering bulbs, such as crocus, can provide a carpet of color from midwinter until mid-spring.*

Anemone blanda

This is a popular winter- and spring-flowering plant with a low, spreading habit, reaching no more than 6in (15cm) high. The flowers have from 10 to 15 long, narrow tepals (modified petals) borne singly on short green stems, with flower colors varying from deep blue, through shades of pink, to pure white. The leaves are deep green with a broadly triangular shape, divided into three segments. This hardy little plant prefers a well-drained soil with plenty of organic matter and will grow well in full sun or partial shade. In very hard winters, it can be protected with a mulch of organic matter, which it will then grow through and produce its flowers. There are a number of selected flower forms that produce single colors, including *Anemone blanda* 'Blue Star' with light blue flowers; *A. b.* 'Radar', white and magenta; and *A. b.* 'White Splendor', which has pure white blooms. ✽ ✽ ✽ ✽ ✽

Plant at least 2in (5cm) deep during late summer or early fall in a moist, well-drained soil. Tends to be prone to leaf spot and powdery mildew.

Chionodoxa luciliae

This is a small group of hardy bulbs originating from Turkey and its surrounding area, with the common name of glory of the snow. In late winter and early spring, short spikes up to 6in (15cm) high are produced, carrying groups of up to three small, star-shaped flowers, which are mid-blue in color, with a dark blue line and white markings at the base of each petal. The short, narrow leaves are mid-green in color and arranged in pairs around the base of the green flower stem. There are a number of single-colored forms now available, such as the pure white *Chionodoxa luciliae* 'Alba' and the pink-flowered form *C. l.* 'Rosea'. However, there is some confusion over plant naming and *Chionodoxa luciliae* may also be sold as *C. gigantea* or *C. forbesii.* ✽ ✽ ✽ ✽

Plant bulbs 3in (8cm) deep during fall. This plant will grow best in a sunny position, but prefers a fertile, well-drained soil.

Crocus chrysanthus

There are many hardy crocus hybrids related to *Crocus chrysanthus* that flower in late winter and early spring, with short, dull gray to mid-green leaves up to 2in (5cm) long. Each plant can produce up to four flowers. There are some truly outstanding early flowering cultivars within this group, and many are so reliable that no winter garden should be without at least one cultivar positioned somewhere.

A very free-flowering cultivar is *Crocus chrysanthus* 'Cream Beauty', which has rich cream flowers, with pale greenish brown coloring at the base and golden yellow markings on the inside. A stunning blue-flowered cultivar is *C. c.* 'Princess Beatrix', which has mid-blue petals and a golden yellow base to the flower, while *C. c.* 'Snow Bunting' is a delicate white, with faint purple markings on the outside of each petal, a golden orange throat, and bright orange style and stigma in the center of the flower.

This group of plants is suitable for forcing indoors, and after flowering can be planted out to naturalize in the garden. They all prefer very similar growing conditions: They must have a soil that is well drained, although they do not require a lot of feeding and will often grow well in poor, impoverished soils. Growing in an open, sunny position suits them well, and they make excellent plants for naturalizing in lawns and south-facing mixed borders, where they will often form large colonies once they have established.

These plants may need some protection while they are in flower, not from the cold but from birds. Some birds will peck at the flowers and tear them to shreds, often leaving small segments of petals scattered around the base of each plant. Thin cotton or a fine mesh netting suspended just above the flowers will help to deter the birds without detracting from the beauty of the blooms. ✽ ✽ ✽ ✽

It is best to plant spring-flowering crocus during fall, 3–4in (8–10cm) deep in the soil and equally spaced apart. May require protection from rodents and birds.

TOP *The common name, glory of the snow, is an indication of the time of year when* Chionodoxa luciliae *is likely to flower.*

ABOVE RIGHT Crocus chrysanthus *'Princess Beatrix' has stunning mid-blue flowers with a splash of yellow at the base of each petal.*

ABOVE *With its yellow flowers,* Crocus chysanthus *'Cream Beauty' is one of the most free-flowering winter crocuses.*

RIGHT *Some forms of the handsome* Anemone blanda, *such as the large-flowered 'White Splendor', start to flower from midwinter onward.*

Crocus tommasinianus

This hardy crocus reaches up to 4in (10cm) in height, and produces one or two slender flowers from each corm. The flowers come out in January/February. To protect from mice, squirrels, and birds, place a frame with wire netting over the plants when in flower. Flower color varies from silvery lilac through to shades of deep reddish mauve; outer tepals are often overlaid silver. The petals start in tight cups and open to a flat, water lily-like shape. There is also a form with pure white flowers, *C. tommasinianus* f. *albus*. Both will grow equally well in a sunny position or partial shade, but prefer a fertile, well-drained soil in full sun. An excellent choice for naturalizing in woodland or lawns, they look best planted densely in a sweep of color and also work well at the front of borders, in rock gardens, and in tubs and other containers. Not suitable for cutting. Recommended varieties include 'Ruby Giant' and 'Whitewell Purple'. ❄ ❄ ❄ ❄ ❄

Plant corms during fall, placing them 3–4in (8–10cm) deep and apart. Lift and divide every few years as necessary.

Cyclamen coum

Hardy cyclamen are incredibly tough little perennial plants, with almost round or broadly oval-shaped leaves held up on curling red stems. Although they are treated by many gardeners as a bulb, they are in fact a corm and prefer to grow on or just below soil level. Many species have pronounced silver or gray markings on their dark-green leaves. *Cyclamen coum* reaches only 3in (8cm) high and produces delicate flowers in shades of pink through to carmine-red in the depths of winter, often all growing together in the same group or "colony," while *C. hederifolium* grows up to 5in (12cm) high and bears pink flowers with maroon markings in late fall and early winter. ❄ ❄ ❄ ❄ ❄ ❄

Plant 1¼–2in (3–5cm) deep in a dry, shaded place, such as close to the base of a tree. Propagation is by seed sown as soon as it is ripe.

Eranthis hyemalis

The winter aconite is valued for its early flowering, and although it is treated as a bulb, it is actually a tuberous, hardy perennial, with attractive pale green, deeply cut leaves. In late winter and early spring, small, yellow, buttercup-like flowers appear, ¾–1¼in (2–3cm) across, with a green frill of leaves held above the ground on a green, 4in (10cm) high stem. Aconites prefer a moist, well-drained soil and a shaded or semishaded woodland situation. They can be divided in the spring immediately after the flowers have died and replanted to a depth of 2in (5cm) and about 4in (10cm) apart. Wear gloves when handling tubers/plants as contact with the sap may irritate skin. ❄ ❄ ❄ ❄ ❄

Plant tubers 2in (5cm) deep during fall. The plants spread and self-seed freely, forming large colonies in alkaline soil. Lift and divide the tubers in spring after flowering. Slugs may eat the foliage.

Galanthus elwesii

Commonly referred to as the giant snowdrop because it is much more vigorous than the ordinary snowdrop, this popular plant is one of a genus of small, hardy, clump-forming bulbs. They are grown for their pure white, honey-scented flowers flecked with green and produced in February and March. *Galanthus elwesii* are usually carried singly on a slender green stalk, up to 10in (25cm) in length. The 4–6in (10–15cm) long flat, strap-shaped leaves are a dull gray-green, often with a slightly bluish sheen to them, and arranged in pairs, usually on either side of the flower stalk. This plant prefers a well-drained, moisture-retentive soil and must never be allowed to dry out while growing. It thrives in partial shade under trees and shrubs, which makes it a perfect choice for naturalizing. ❄ ❄ ❄ ❄ ❄

Propagate by dividing the clumps immediately after flowering, while the leaves are still green.

LEFT Crocus tommasinianus *is among the earliest of the winter-flowering crocus and is an ideal choice for naturalizing in lawns or shaded areas.*

BELOW Galanthus elwesii *is one of the largest of the true snowdrops. The white flowers have a characteristic green marking on their inner petals.*

BOTTOM RIGHT *Hardy cyclamen make excellent plants for the winter garden, flowering before and after Christmas.*

BOTTOM LEFT *The green foliage of winter aconite (*Eranthis hyemalis*) remains long after the flowers have faded.*

Galanthus nivalis

Commonly known as the snowdrop, this pretty perennial is incredibly hardy, its flowers appearing early in the year. There is a huge variety of species of snowdrop available. *Galanthus nivalis* produces white, dangling, bell-like flowers, often with an inverted V-shaped green mark at the tip of each inner tepal, on 8in (20cm) stems among the narrow, straplike, deep-green leaves in the depths of winter. The flowers are sweetly scented. Snowdrops prefer a moist but well-drained soil, and will rapidly colonize areas under trees or in lawns once established. They also grow well in borders and rock gardens. Snowdrops do not transplant well if the bulbs are allowed to dry out. Contact with the bulbs may irritate skin. Recommended varieties include 'Flore Pleno'. ※ ※ ※ ※

For best results, snowdrops should be planted about 3in (8cm) deep, immediately after flowering has finished in early spring. Plant thickly to give the best effect. Prone to narcissus bulb fly and gray mold.

Iris reticulata

This is a hardy, bulb-forming iris from the large Reticulata group of plants, which flower from late winter through to mid-spring. The mid-green leaves are square-sectioned, up to 4in (10cm) in length, and narrowing to a point at the tip. The flowers are carried singly on short, green 4–6in (10–15cm) high stems, in colors varying from reddish purple through deep violet-blue to pale violet-blue. All the color variations have yellow markings on the petals. There are now many named cultivars of *Iris reticulata* and one of the most outstanding is 'Katharine Hodgkin', with pale blue flowers delicately patterned with yellow and dark-blue markings on the petals. These plants prefer an alkaline soil that is moist and fertile, but free-draining, with plenty of sunlight. ※ ※ ※ ※ ※

Plant Reticulata bulbs 2–4in (5–10cm) apart. After flowering they will divide into several small bulbs, which may take several years to grow and develop before they start to flower.

Leucojum vernum var. vagneri

Commonly called the spring snowflake, this early flowering hardy bulb is often mistaken for a snowdrop, although it produces a much taller flower stem, 8–10in (20–25cm) high, and the flowers are much larger. The leaves are thick and straplike, dark glossy green in color, and grow around the base of a dark-green stem that carries two bell-shaped flowers, held just above the leaves. Each flower is pure white with a green spot on the tip of each petal. The variety *Leucojum vernum var. vagneri*, is much more robust than the more common *L. vernum*, and there is also an *L. v. var. carpathicum*, which has yellow tips to the petals rather than the more usual green. This bulb will grow well in damp soil close to a stream or pool and is a good choice for naturalized planting. It provides an interesting effect when used in mixed plantings with snowdrops. ※ ※ ※ ※ ※

Plant dry bulbs in a moist, humus-rich soil. Will grow well in full sun if the soil is kept moist. Prone to slugs and narcissus bulb fly.

Narcissus bulbocodium

Another popular flower, daffodils are grown for their attractive spring flowers. *Narcissus bulbocodium* is a distinctive, hardy, dwarf species of narcissus, commonly known as the hoop-petticoat daffodil. The wide, rich-yellow, funnel-shaped flowers with narrow petals are produced singly in mid-spring, among dark-green, narrow, straplike leaves that are up to 6in (15cm) long. This plant will grow well in a sunny position or in partial shade. It prefers a moist, well-drained soil and is an excellent choice for naturalizing in ornamental lawns or meadow areas, or adding to a rock garden. It can be naturalized in damp grassland, which dries out in the summer, but avoid mowing the grass until after the flower has shed its seeds. ※ ※ ※ ※ ※ ※

Plant bulbs to a depth of 3–4in (8–10cm) and about 6in (15cm) apart in September or October. Problems include large narcissus bulb fly, narcissus eelworm, slugs, narcissus basal rot, and other fungal infections.

TOP Narcissus bulbocodium *produces rather unusual, tubular flowers on slender green stalks and is a popular bulb for planting in rock gardens.*

ABOVE RIGHT Iris *'Katharine Hodgkin' is an extremely popular cultivar, which has delicate blue flowers with a tracery of yellow and blue markings on the petals.*

ABOVE *The snowdrop (*Galanthus nivalis*) is one of the plants most commonly associated with the winter months. The blooms are honey-scented, a fact that is seldom appreciated because they are so low-growing.*

RIGHT *Although this plant is often mistaken for the snowdrop,* Leucojum vernum *var.* vagneri *is larger and produces two dangling, bell-shaped flowers from each stem in late winter or early spring.*

Narcissus papyraceus

Often called the paper white narcissus, and even sold as *Narcissus* 'Paper White', this plant is grouped into division 8 (Tazetta daffodils) of the Narcissus classification. It usually grows to a height of 16in (40cm) and has long, broad, mid-green leaves, held very erect above ground level. In the center of each group of leaves is a round, mid-green flower stem that carries up to 10 clear white flowers, which are very fragrant. Although a winter-flowering plant, it is not as hardy as some species and benefits from the provision of some shelter, such as growing in a south-facing border or under trees so that a small amount of frost protection is provided. These plants will grow in a wide range of soil types providing they are well drained. They prefer a sunny position and are excellent for naturalizing in lawns or mixed borders. ❄ ❄ ❄ ❄ ❄ ❄ ❄

Propagate by dividing offsets after the foliage has died down. Avoid growing in waterlogged soils, as this encourages fungal rots.

Scilla mischtschenkoana

Originally known as *Scilla tubergeniana*, but now changed to the almost unpronounceable *S. mischtschenkoana*, this plant originates from Iran and is often mistaken for *S. siberica*. It is slightly taller than *S. siberica*, reaching 4–8in (10–20cm) in height, with pale blue flowers; each petal has a deep-blue stripe along its center and each flower opens almost flat in the bright winter sun. The flowers will start to emerge as soon as the leaves and buds push through the soil, and flowering will continue until the stems have reached their full height. This is an excellent plant, ideal for raised beds or rock gardens. It also grows well when naturalized in a semishaded border under trees and shrubs. It must have a well-drained but moisture-retentive soil in order to grow well. ❄ ❄ ❄ ❄ ❄

Propagation is by division of the bulb clump in the fall, but they must be replanted immediately.

Scilla siberica

Commonly called the Siberian squill, this close relative of the English bluebell is a low-growing hardy little bulb and reaches 2–6in (5–15cm) in height. It is grown for its nodding, bell-like flowers, which are produced in late winter or early spring. The flowers start to emerge as soon as the leaves and buds push through the cold winter soil, and flowering continues for several weeks. The flowers are usually brilliant blue in color but there are a number of named cultivars with differing flower colors, such as *Scilla siberica* 'Alba' with pure white flowers and *S. s.* 'Spring Beauty' with deep-blue blooms. This is an excellent flowering bulb, ideal for rock gardens or raised beds, and equally happy as a naturalized plant in a border under deciduous shrubs. ❄ ❄ ❄ ❄ ❄

To propagate these bulbs, lift and divide them at four- to five-year intervals, in late summer or early fall.

Tulipa humilis

This dwarf species of early flowering tulip grows to no more than 3–6in (8–15cm) tall. It originates from areas of Iran and Turkey. The narrow leaves are a grayish green color and form a flattish rosette just above ground level. From the center of the rosette, a stout grayish green stem is produced, which is topped with a magenta-pink flower with a golden yellow center. This is a very variable species with distinct changes in both habit and flower color, depending on the geographic location from which the parent plants were collected. As a result, this plant has a variant, *Tulipa humilis* var. *pulchella*, and more variation called *T. h.* var. *pulchella* 'Violacea Group'. However, there are some outstanding named cultivars of *T. humilis*: 'Persian Pearl' has cyclamen-purple flowers with yellow markings at the base; 'Odalisque' is light purple with a yellow base; and 'Eastern Star' is rose-pink with bronze and green markings. ❄ ❄ ❄ ❄

Propagation is by lifting the parent bulb and removing any offsets after the foliage has died down. Gray squirrels may eat the plants.

ABOVE LEFT Scilla mischtschenkoana
is much favored as an early-flowering
bulb for rock gardens or raised beds.

TOP Narcissus papyraceus (the paper
white daffodil) is an early-flowering
bulb that produces clear white flowers.

ABOVE Scilla siberica is a resilient plant
that can be used to naturalize in borders.
Left undisturbed, it is capable of
colonizing large areas of the garden.

LEFT Tulipa humilis 'Lilliput' is one of
a group of low-growing but very free-
flowering tulips, ideal for naturalizing.

perennials

The most common botanical description for a herbaceous perennial is a plant that has an annual top that lasts for one year and a perennial root system and storage organs that will last for many years. Yet within this group of plants there are a number that are actually evergreen, and their tough, leathery leaves will provide a welcome touch of winter greenery. Some perennials produce a good winter-flowering display, and others make a decorative contribution with lingering fruits or flower heads to provide interest through the shortest days of the year.

It is not common to think of perennials as bearing interesting fruits, least of all through the winter months, but there are some that do. The most notable is the Chinese lantern (*Physalis alkekengi* var. *franchetii*), which develops an orange-red, papery calyx, surrounding a cherrylike fruit. These structures hang on the plant in winter, with the outer "lantern" bobbing in the wind and gradually disintegrating to reveal the ripened berry inside.

The parts of plants that are dead can provide sound as well as visual impact. The nodding seed heads or remains of flowers will often linger on ornamental grasses throughout winter, perhaps moving gently on the breeze or arched over in defiance of the chill winter winds. Even when conditions are still and quiet, there are still some striking effects—on cold, icy days the formation of ice crystals over these structures can be visually stunning.

On some perennials the leaves form the decorative feature. The large, rounded leaves of bergenia earn the common name of elephant's ears, while some hellebores have spiky, almost palmlike leaves. Others, such as the epimediums, have tough leaves, with a deceptively delicate appearance. The long, straplike leaves of daylilies (*Hemerocallis*) can also bring welcome relief to the barren earth in winter. Often, tints of bronze, orange, and purple will develop on the leaf margins as winter really sets in.

Some perennials are not tough enough to keep their leaves throughout winter, but others are hardy enough to produce a display of flowers. Hellebores offer a range of colors, from purples to yellows and pure whites. Bergenias have, on the whole, smaller flowers, but they make up for their lack of size with tight clusters of white and pink blooms on short, red stems.

RIGHT Pulmonaria saccharata *produces pinkish red flowers in late winter. The flowers change from mauve to a rich blue as they age.*

LEFT Helleborus orientalis *produces cup-shaped flowers through the depths of winter and into spring, often emerging to flower through a deep covering of snow.*

BELOW LEFT Pulmonaria 'Sissinghurst White' *is one of the more vigorous plants, with flowers that start as pale pink buds and open to pure white.*

BELOW *Perennials provide a rich variety of color and form, creating interest in any season, including winter when their old stems and flower heads provide color.*

Bergenia crassifolia

This is a hardy, clump-forming, evergreen perennial with bold, tough, leathery leaves that are rounded with a heart-shaped base and toothed leaf margins. They are mid-green in color, becoming attractive in the winter when orange and yellow tints are found on the leaf edges. The changes in leaf color are more pronounced when the plants are grown on poor soils, especially in exposed positions. In late winter and early spring, bell-shaped, pinkish purple flowers are arranged in drooping heads, carried above the leaves on erect branching stems 18in (45cm) tall, which are often tinted red. *Bergenia crassifolia* var. *pacifica* has larger leaves and produces reddish purple flowers on 1ft (30cm) stems through the late-winter months. This hardy plant is excellent for ground cover and will grow equally well in full sun or partially shaded conditions. The common name for this plant is elephant's ears. ✳ ✳ ✳

Propagate by division in late spring after flowering. Leaf color is improved by planting in full sun.

Epimedium x warleyense

These low-growing, clump-forming, hardy evergreen, or in some cases semievergreen, plants are superb as ground cover for growing in conditions of full or partial shade. In fact, trees will help to protect the plants if weather conditions become very severe. The leaves are almost heart-shaped and are bright green, tinted pinkish red when young, darkening with age. In fall and winter, these leaves display vivid tints of yellow, orange, red, and bronze, carried on thin woody leaf stalks up to 1ft (30cm) high. The clusters of small, cup-shaped flowers, which give the plant its common name of the bishop's hat, are bright orange and produced in spring and summer, although flowers can be produced in colors ranging from yellow to mauve, depending on the cultivar. ✳ ✳ ✳ ✳

These plants may suffer from severe leaf scorch if they are planted in an open situation and subjected to very bright summer sunlight. Propagation is by division in early spring.

Helleborus orientalis

Commonly known as the Lenten rose, this hardy evergreen perennial forms a compact mound of tough, leathery leaves, which are mid-green to dark green in color on the upper surface, but much paler on the underside. The leaves are carried on thick, hollow, pale green stems reaching up to 18ft (45cm) in height, often lying over onto the ground as they reach their full height to make room for new leaves or flowers emerging from the center of the clump. In winter, each flower head is made up of several cup-shaped, white or creamy-green blooms, some with red or pinkish markings, produced at the shoot tip. There are a number of yellow-flowered cultivars now available, such as *Helleborus orientalis* 'Lemon Yellow'. Cut back the stems after flowering has finished to prune the plant. ✳ ✳ ✳ ✳ ✳ ✳

Propagation is by seed sown in the summer and placed in a cold frame, or by division for most of the named cultivars.

Iris unguicularis

This vigorous, clump-forming iris spreads through the soil by means of underground stems (rhizomes) and reaches a height of 16in (40cm). The narrow, grasslike leaves will grow up to 2ft (60cm) long but can look untidy as the tips often die and turn brown. In late winter and early spring the short green stems carry single flowers, which are a lavender-violet color with yellow, white, and purple markings. Often a flush of smaller flowers will be produced in a short burst in the fall. There are a number of single-colored cultivars, including *Iris unguicularis* 'Alba', which has white flowers with yellow markings, although this is less hardy than the darker-colored forms. *I. u.* 'Mary Barnard' has deep-violet flowers in midwinter and *I. u.* 'Walter Butt' produces pale lavender blooms in early to midwinter. These plants prefer a well-drained neutral to alkaline soil in full sun. ✳ ✳ ✳ ✳

These plants are propagated by division. To keep them vigorous and healthy, lift and divide every third or fourth year.

RIGHT *Although epimedium does not flower in winter, the heart-shaped leaves turn copper-colored in cold weather and sparkle under a dusting of frost.*

BELOW RIGHT *Bergenias provide good leaf color as well as flowers, often responding to the cold by showing reddish purple markings on their glossy green leaves.*

BELOW Iris unguicularis *will usually produce a regular succession of flowers through the winter months rather than one short, intense burst of color.*

BOTTOM *Hellebores are closely associated with winter gardens, with their angular foliage and tough long-lasting flowers, available in a range of colors.*

Physalis alkekengi var. franchetii

A close relative of the potato, and commonly called the Chinese lantern plant, this straggly, spreading, hardy herbaceous perennial is a deciduous plant with thin, mid-green leaves held on pale green stems. The main attraction is the orange, papery capsules, which have an edible, reddish orange berry within. These lantern-like fruits, which stand about 2½ft (75cm) above the ground, will remain on the plant all winter, dangling in the breeze long after the leaves have died. Once established, this plant may become invasive and spread quickly through the soil by means of long, white underground stems called rhizomes. There is a very attractive low-growing cultivar called 'Zwerg' ('Dwarf') that is far less vigorous. ❋ ❋ ❋ ❋ ❋ ❋

This plant will grow in almost any soil, provided it is not too dry, but it will need to be cut down to ground level each spring.

Pulmonaria

Commonly known as lungwort, this shade-loving hardy plant is one of the earliest to flower in the late winter and early spring. It is an excellent ground-cover plant and has beautiful foliage. The broadly oval-shaped leaves are usually a mid-green color, sometimes variegated with silvery gray spots flecked evenly over the upper surface of the leaf, which is often covered with a layer of fine hairs. The trumpet-shaped flowers are held above the leaves on short hairy flower stalks, in color shades ranging from blue to red, pink, or white. There are numerous species, hybrids, and cultivars available, and often their flowers will change color as they age. *Pulmonaria longifolia* has very narrow, spotted leaves and bright blue flowers; the cultivar 'Lewis Palmer' has broader, spotted foliage and soft, blue blossoms, which turn pink later. ❋ ❋ ❋ ❋ ❋ ❋

These plants must have a deep soil with plenty of moisture, as they are very sensitive to mildew on the leaves when grown in dry soil.

Stipa gigantea

Known as the giant feather grass, this is a hardy evergreen grass, forming a dense, tufted mound of long, narrow, rolled leaves, mid-green in color and often up to 2½ft (75cm) long. Although this plant flowers in the summer, when it produces long slender stems carrying large oat-like flowers up to 6ft (2m) above the ground; these flowers will turn golden as they age, lasting on the plant throughout the winter. This plant looks particularly stunning in winter when covered with a coating of ice crystals following an overnight frost. It looks good when grown against a background of darker-leaved plants and is excellent for growing as a specimen. ❋ ❋ ❋

Needs plenty of space, and prefers a free-draining soil and plenty of sunlight. Prune by cutting down the flower stems in spring.

Stipa tenuissima

This plant has a narrow, erect habit, forming a clump of about 1ft (30cm) across and up to 20in (50cm) in height. Throughout the summer, it produces masses of soft flower spikes up to 12in (30cm) long, which are held above the leaves. The delicate flower heads start out greenish white in color, turning to the golden yellow shades of straw as they age and nodding gently in the breeze. This hardy deciduous grass will stay attractive throughout the winter even though the flowers are dead. The long, narrow, bright green leaves are tightly rolled and reach up to 16in (40cm) in length. The plant is a native of the southeastern United States and northern South America. It is capable of withstanding long periods of time without much water. The leaves and flower stalks can be used in dried flower arrangements. This is a plant that will grow in most well-drained soils, but prefers bright sunlight. ❋ ❋ ❋ ❋ ❋ ❋ ❋

Propagation is by seed sown in the spring under protection, but to get large plants quickly, the preferred method is by division in late spring or early summer.

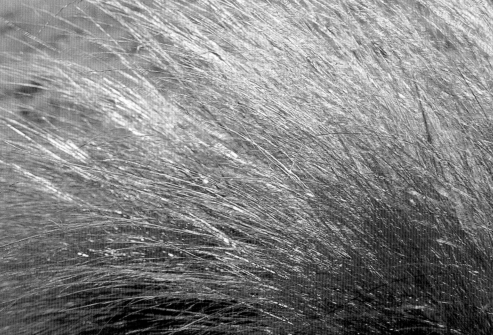

TOP LEFT *In winter only the orange fruits of the Chinese lantern (*Physalis alkekengi *var.* franchetii) *remain, on brown stems.*

TOP Stipa tenuifolia, *or feather grass, has straw-colored leaves that make a rustling sound in the wind.*

ABOVE *Commonly known as lungwort,* Pulmonaria longifolia *has narrow, spotted leaves and blue-purple flowers.*

LEFT Stipa gigantea *is often referred to as an architectural plant due to its dominant stature. The dead flower heads add height and movement to the winter garden.*

climbers

Climbers can be confusing as a group of plants because they are often classed separately, even though the plant in question may simply be a climbing version of a plant from a different group. The terms used to classify them may also be misleading. Wall shrubs get mixed up with climbers because of the way they are grown, and plants such as climbing roses are not, in reality, climbers at all. True climbing plants have their own method of self-support, be it tendrils, twining stems, aerial roots, sucker pods, or twining leaf stalks.

If the plant does not possess any of these methods of supporting itself, it is technically a wall shrub and will need to be trained and tied into place. Climbing plants and wall shrubs are increasing in popularity as gardens become smaller and the pressure on space increases. There is a tendency toward vertical gardening, growing the plants upward because there is less room to garden outward.

As a framework within the garden, evergreen climbing plants can be valuable, especially if something needs to be hidden. The offending item is more likely to be seen during winter when there is less foliage, and this is where the evergreen plants come into their own, particularly if the plants chosen have foliage that is variegated with silver and gold tints to create more interest. Variegated ivy will cover walls and fences, and the wide range of leaf shapes and colors will draw attention to the plant rather than what it is growing over. Wildlife will appreciate the cover, using the plants for shelter on winter nights, as well as the food that the plants provide in the form of the black fruits.

Many evergreen plants will also flower and produce attractive, brightly colored fruits—a bonus to anyone planning a winter garden. The fern-leaf clematis, with its creamy-yellow flowers, which open all winter long, always look attractive no matter how adverse the weather conditions become.

Plants grown as wall shrubs can also produce a stunning winter display of color. Winter jasmine produces yellow flowers almost all winter long, and the berries of the firethorn (*Pyracantha*) attract attention with their shades of red and yellow. Other, less common, plants include *Clematis napaulensis*, a deciduous plant with small, creamy-yellow, bell-shaped flowers, which have a purple center to them. This plant produces flowers in the depths of winter.

RIGHT *Parthenocissus are grown for their attractive, brightly colored leaves. Grow to cover a wall or fence.*

FAR RIGHT AND BELOW *If there is one climbing plant that you can rely on to flower in winter, it is the winter jasmine* (Jasminum nudiflorum), *which produces a succession of flowers in small flushes rather than one short burst of color.*

BELOW RIGHT *Clematis armandii is an outstanding evergreen clematis with glossy green leaves and fragrant white, star-like flowers. It can be slow to establish, but is worth the wait.*

Clematis cirrhosa var. balearica

This vigorous, reliable plant is one of the easiest climbers to grow because it will survive almost anywhere and produce an excellent display. The four-petaled flowers are a pale yellowish color, with purple markings inside, emerging from late fall to early spring. They are followed by silky tufted seed heads. Often called the fern-leaved clematis because of its finely cut evergreen foliage, in winter the thin green shoots and leaves will often turn a dull bronze color as the weather becomes cooler. A mature plant will eventually reach 10ft (3m) in height. There are also two cultivars that are often grown: 'Freckles', with much deeper and more frequent flower markings, and 'Wisley Cream', with larger, paler colored flowers and very few markings. No regular pruning is required for any of these clematis. ❄ ❄ ❄ ❄ ❄ ❄ ❄

This plant is easy to grow from cuttings and appears resistant to most pests and diseases.

Hedera colchica 'Sulfur Heart'

This is an impressive self-clinging climber, supporting itself with aerial roots. It has large evergreen leaves, three-lobed or broadly oval in shape, and each leaf is boldly marked with an irregular central splash of gold, surrounded by pale green and a deeper green around the leaf margins. This is a hardy, vigorous plant with light green stems that will soon reach a height of 15ft (5m) and spread 25–30ft (8–10m) over a wall or panel fence within a few years. It is often called the golden Persian ivy and will grow in a wide range of soils, although it prefers a fertile soil with plenty of organic matter and some free lime. This plant is also sold under other (inaccurate) names, such as 'Gold Leaf' and 'Paddy's Pride'. This plant requires no regular pruning and is very easy to maintain, although it can be slow to establish and start to climb over a wall or fence. ❄ ❄ ❄ ❄ ❄ ❄ ❄

Propagation is by semi-ripe cuttings, taken in summer, or by layering by pegging shoots down onto the soil.

Hedera helix 'Glacier'

Often referred to as the English ivy, this is a tough, self-clinging plant with a climbing or trailing habit. There are many different cultivars, which are usually selected for their varied leaf shape, leaf color, or both. *Hedera helix* 'Glacier' is one of the most commonly grown cultivars due to its attractively variegated leaves, which are almost triangular in shape and gray-green in color, with silver, gray, and cream markings carried on purple-green stems. Climbing to a height of 10ft (3m) or more, this plant will grow well as a climber or as ground cover. An easy-to-grow, adaptable plant, it was introduced into Europe from California in the 1950s and has become one of the most common garden plants to be grown both indoors and outside. ❄ ❄ ❄ ❄ ❄ ❄

As for Hedera colchica, *propagation is by semi-ripe cuttings, taken in summer, or by layering by pegging shoots down onto the soil.*

Jasminum nudiflorum

Commonly known as the winter jasmine, this popular plant is an outstanding winter performer. It can be grown as a freestanding shrub or as a wall shrub. The thin, whippy, almost leafless stems, which can reach up to 10ft (3m) long, are square in shape and green in color, which gives the whole plant an evergreen appearance. It is grown mainly for its small, fragrant, tubular yellow flowers, which open from late fall through until early spring to form a five-petaled star. The variegated form, *Jasminum nudiflorum* 'Aureum', has golden yellow splashes on the leaves. Winter jasmine can be grown in almost any situation and on almost any soil—it is a real survivor and an excellent choice for new gardeners as well as those with more experience. ❄ ❄ ❄ ❄ ❄ ❄

This plant is easy to propagate, either by semi-ripe cuttings taken in September, or by tip layers that occur naturally wherever the stems touch the soil.

LEFT Hedera colchica *'Sulfur Heart'* is an attractive, large-leaved ivy, the perfect choice for a shady corner.

BELOW Jasminum nudiflorum *is a winter "must"—a plant that flowers through winter when others may struggle.*

BOTTOM RIGHT Clematis cirrhosa *var.* balearica *has finely cut, evergreen leaves and pale yellow flowers in winter; it is excellent for hiding unsightly objects.*

BOTTOM LEFT Hedera helix *'Glacier' is a hardy, self-reliant climber that will grow well up a wall or fence, or as ground cover, spreading over beds and borders.*

trees and shrubs

Gardeners, without realizing it, often display a tendency to select trees and shrubs that act as nature's demarcation points by signaling the beginning or end of a season. The perfect illustration of this is the popularity of plants that display fall color in the garden, often seen as a significant marker to show the growing year is drawing to an end. At the opposite end of the scale, a bold display of flowering cherries is seen by many as a sign that nature is waking from its slumbers and spring's great adventure is about to begin.

In summer, there is often so much going on in the garden that most trees and shrubs become part of the overall scheme, and all but the unusual or truly outstanding either go unnoticed or are rarely fully appreciated. This is what makes the winter so special, as some trees and shrubs save their best display for the shortest days of the year.

Colored stems provide their own display, from the flaking bark of the paper-bark maple (*Acer griseum*), river birch (*Betula nigra*), and Manchurian cherry (*Prunus maackii*) to the peeling bark of the Himalayan birch (*Betula utilis*) and the birch-bark cherry (*Prunus serrula*). The bright stems of redtwig dogwood (*Cornus alba*) and willow (*Salix* spp.) are well known, but the striped bark of the snake-bark maples (*Acer capillipes*, *A. davidii*, and *A. pensylvanicum*) are just as attractive, if less common.

Many more woody plants will carry their brightly colored fruits through the winter. Cotoneaster, hawthorn (*Crataegus* spp.), holly (*Ilex*), rose (*Rosa* spp.), and many others will often offer winter displays of red, orange, or yellow berries, which often far exceed the flower display that preceded them.

Conifers and broad-leaved evergreens give structure to any garden, with attractive silver, golden, and variegated foliage. Some plants respond to the cold weather by turning shades of orange and coppery bronze on the tips of the youngest shoots, including many of the Scotch heathers (*Calluna vulgaris*), with one called *C. v.* 'Winter Chocolate', which provides outstanding winter foliage color. All of this is in addition to those shrubs and trees that flower, with chimonanthus, hamamelis, lonicera, mahonia, and prunus providing color, fragrance, and interest through winter's bleak, short days.

RIGHT *The white coating on the stems of* Rubus cockburnianus *flakes off to reveal wine-red stems beneath.*

ABOVE LEFT *Viburnum tinus is an evergreen shrub with glossy green leaves. It has clusters of pink buds, which open white, followed by blue-black fruits.*

CENTER *Sarcococcas are low-growing shrubs with dense, suckering growth, ideal for growing near a path.*

CENTER RIGHT *Viburnum farreri is a mildly hardy shrub producing clusters of fragrant, pink-flushed white flowers.*

BELOW RIGHT *Corylus avellana 'Contorta' bears attractive catkins in late winter and early spring.*

Acer griseum

This is a tough plant that forms an attractive, slow-growing tree and will eventually reach 20ft (6.5m) in height. It has unusual leaves (for a maple), which are divided into three sections. They are dark green in color on the upper surface and blue-green on the underside, turning red and scarlet in the fall, with some leaves hanging on young trees all winter. The most interesting virtue of this tree is displayed through the winter when the copper-colored bark rolls off in large pieces to reveal light, orange-brown new bark beneath, earning it the nickname paper-bark maple. In the spring, inconspicuous flowers are produced, followed by winged, gray-green fruits that are covered in soft, downy felt. This plant is usually difficult to propagate, but seed sown in the fall is the method most likely to be successful. ❄ ❄ ❄ ❄ ❄

This tree is slow to establish and will benefit from some shelter and protection for the first few years after planting.

Betula

These attractive deciduous trees, many of which are extremely hardy (ranging from zone 1 to zone 9 depending on the species), have something to offer the garden all year round. Delicate yellow-brown catkins are produced in the spring; in the summer, the oval-shaped, dark-green leaves offer light-dappled shade in the garden, turning a golden butter-yellow before being shed in the fall. Throughout the winter and early spring, the peeling bark of the trunk and main branches makes an outstanding sight. The range of bark colors on the stem can vary considerably, depending on the species: *Betula albosinensis* has bark with a coppery-pink tinge, *B. alleghaniensis* has amber-colored bark, and the most commonly grown of all, *B. pendula* (the silver birch), has silvery-white bark and is often referred to as the lady of the woods. ❄

Propagation is by seed sown outdoors in the fall, or by cuttings taken in the summer.

Chimonanthus praecox

The wintersweet is one of the truly outstanding winter-flowering shrubs. It has tough, waxy flowers, which have narrow petals colored a pale translucent yellow with a purple center, opening from midwinter onward. An added bonus with this plant is the delicate, spicy fragrance produced by the flowers. The cultivar *Chimonanthus praecox* 'Grandiflorus' has larger flowers of a deeper golden yellow, but the fragrance is much weaker. Although hardy to zone 7, this large, upright shrub is slow to establish, and it may take a number of years before flowers are produced. Grown as a free-standing shrub, it will reach 12ft (4m) in height and 10ft (3m) across, but for smaller gardens it can be trained against a wall. This shrub will grow in most fertile, well-drained soils, but it needs to be in full sun, so that the young branches mature and do not suffer from frost damage. ❄ ❄ ❄ ❄ ❄

This plant can be propagated by bending the lower branches down onto the soil and layering them.

Choisya ternata

This shrub produces dense clusters of small, white, fragrant flowers, earning it the common name of the Mexican orange blossom. It flowers twice a year in spring and late summer. Glossy, evergreen leaves are produced in whorls on green woody stems, forming a densely packed bush up to 6ft (2m) high, with a compact, dome-shaped habit. An adaptable shrub capable of growing in a wide range of soils, it is ideal for a low-maintenance garden, as it needs no regular pruning, although young shoots may be damaged by frost. *Choisya ternata* 'Sundance' is a popular cultivar, with bright yellow foliage that turns lime-green as it ages, making it stand out in winter when other plants have shed their leaves. This plant keeps its color better when grown in full sun. The yellow-leaved cultivar is less hardy than the green form. ❄ ❄ ❄ ❄ ❄ ❄

Propagation is by semi-ripe cuttings in late spring or fall.

BELOW *The paper-bark maple (Acer griseum) is an outstanding tree, with attractive, peeling, orange-brown bark.*

RIGHT *A versatile shrub, Choisya ternata 'Sundance' has dark evergreen leaves and white, fragrant, star-shaped flowers. It will grow in a variety of soils and conditions.*

BOTTOM RIGHT *Betula albosinensis var. septentrionalis is a conically shaped tree, grown for its handsome bark.*

BOTTOM *Wintersweet (Chimonanthus praecox) is one of the most strongly scented winter-flowering shrubs available, with a wonderful spicy fragrance.*

Cornus mas

The Cornelian cherry is a hardy plant that will form a small tree or large shrub reaching up to 15ft (5m) in height and spreading at least the same distance outward. The small, yellow, fragrant blossoms open in the depths of winter, forming tight, golden yellow clusters held close to the naked, twiggy branches, and will continue to open well into the spring. By mid-spring, broadly oval-shaped, mid-green, glossy leaves are produced in opposite pairs along the branches after the flowers have faded. There are several different cultivars of this plant, which are less vigorous and provide additional interest at other times of the year: Cornus mas 'Aurea' has pale yellow leaves that gradually turn green as they age and C. m. 'Variegata' has gray-green leaves with a broad, white margin. This plant needs little or no pruning other than removing any dead, damaged, or diseased wood. ✳ ✳ ✳ ✳ ✳

Growing well in a wide range of soils and preferring a sunny position, this makes an excellent specimen for a winter garden.

Cotoneaster lacteus

This is a large, spreading shrub that will eventually reach about 8ft (2.5m) in height and spread to over 10ft (3m), forming a dense thicket of twiggy growth. The thin, drooping twigs are clad with broadly oval-shaped leaves, which are a dull, olive grayish green above and covered with a layer of fine, gray hairs on the underside. Milky-white flowers are produced in broad, flat-topped clusters from early summer, followed by clusters of small, orange-red berries that will last throughout the fall and winter. This plant is well suited as a hedge, either clipped to a formal shape or allowed to grow informally, or it will grow quite happily as a wall shrub on a north- or east-facing wall. Prune by trimming back unwanted shoots after flowering. ✳ ✳ ✳ ✳ ✳ ✳

Most cotoneasters prefer an open, sunny position on a free-draining soil.

Elaeagnus pungens

These tough shrubs are suitable for exposed sites and tolerant of both atmospheric pollution and maritime conditions. The smal, white, highly scented flowers are produced in large numbers well into the winter. The evergreen leaves are broadly oval-shaped with a silvery sheen and thick golden stems. Many types of elaeagnus are grown for their very attractive variegated leaves. Some cultivars of *Elaeagnus pungens* are valuable for providing color all year round. *E. p.* 'Maculata', the most commonly grown, has a vivid golden splash in the center of each deep-green leaf. Closely related are two forms of *E. x ebbingei*, which are also very popular for their attractive variegated leaves: *E. x e.* 'Gilt Edge' has a deep-green leaf with a broad margin of bright golden yellow, and *E. x e.* 'Limelight' leaves start off green and develop a central blotch of golden yellow as they age. ✳ ✳ ✳ ✳ ✳ ✳ ✳

Propagation is by semi-ripe cuttings taken in mid- to late summer.

Erica x darleyensis

The heathers are a large genus of plants, many being natives of Europe, Turkey, and Africa, with the species from the Mediterranean region being particularly hardy. The number of varieties is now large, with new cultivars constantly swelling the ranks of plants available. Their popularity is based on the fact that it is possible to achieve an all-year-round effect when different cultivars are planted. *Erica x darleyensis* and its cultivars are among the easiest to grow and will tolerate a wider range of soils than many heathers. The small bell-like flowers are produced in spikes throughout the winter. *E. x d.* 'Arthur Johnson' produces long spikes of magenta flowers and *E. x d.* 'Silberschmelze' is the best winter white, while *E. x d.* 'Ghost Hills' and 'J.W. Porter' have brightly colored new foliage in the spring. ✳ ✳ ✳ ✳ ✳ ✳

Growing to a height of 2ft (60cm), this plant will spread out to cover about 3ft (1m).

TOP Erica x darleyensis 'J.W. Porter' is
an ideal ground-cover plant, with red
and cream markings on new foliage.

ABOVE RIGHT Cornus mas produces
a mass of yellow flowers in tight, dense
clusters covering the leafless branches.
These are often followed by red fruits.

ABOVE Elaeagnus pungens 'Maculata'
provides a useful framework that provides
color and protection for other plants.

RIGHT Cotoneaster lacteus produces
white flowers in summer, followed by
dense clusters of red fruit.

Hamamelis x intermedia

These are distinctive and beautiful deciduous shrubs reaching up to 10ft (3m) in height. They produce the most attractive of winter displays on the naked branches. *Hamamelis x intermedia* is a hybrid between the Japanese witch hazel (*H. japonica*) and the Chinese witch hazel (*H. mollis*). This plant is quite variable and it is usually named cultivars that are grown. The large leaves are mid-green in color, broadly oval, and provide a stunning display in the fall, turning yellow, orange, scarlet, and red before shedding from the branches. The hardy, frost-resistant flowers have a twisted, spidery appearance, with small, feathery, slightly curled petals, which are mainly colored in various shades of yellow. *H. x i.* 'Sunburst' has pale yellow flowers, but other cultivars have darker-colored flowers. *H. x i.* 'Hiltingbury' has coppery-red, fragrant flowers. ❋ ❋ ❋ ❋ ❋

Propagation is by softwood cuttings in late summer or grafting in midwinter. This plant prefers a slightly acid soil.

Hamamelis mollis

The Chinese witch hazel is a distinctive and beautiful deciduous shrub, which produces one of the most attractive winter displays on its naked branches. The frost-hardy flowers are spidery in appearance, with small straplike petals mainly colored in shades of yellow, but other cultivars have darker-colored flowers. *Hamamelis mollis* 'Brevipetala' has deep yellow flowers and *H. m.* 'Goldcrest' has pale yellow flowers flushed with red. During very cold weather, the petals will curl up tightly and flex open again as the temperature rises. The large mid-green leaves are broadly oval and make a magnificent display in the autumn, turning yellow and copper before falling from the branches. ❋ ❋ ❋ ❋ ❋ ❋

This slow-growing plant prefers partial shade, a slightly acid soil, and a sheltered site. Propagation is by layering softwood cuttings in late summer or grafting in midwinter.

Ilex x altaclerensis 'Golden King'

There are a large number of hardy hollies grown in all types of gardens to form large shrubs or small trees. *Ilex x altaclerensis* 'Golden King' is a popular cultivar because it has attractive green leaves with a golden margin and sharp spines strategically arranged around the leaf edge. In mid- to late spring, inconspicuous, small, white, star-shaped flowers are produced that often go unnoticed, and they are followed by orange-red berries throughout the winter. Hollies will grow in a wide range of soils, providing they are free-draining. They can grow equally well in full sun or partial shade. In spite of its name, *I. x a.* 'Golden King' is a female plant and will produce berries, so it is often grown in association with a male cultivar such as *I. x a.* 'Silver Queen', which has purple young shoots and dark-green leaves with a silver margin. ❋ ❋ ❋ ❋ ❋ ❋

Propagation is by semi-ripe cuttings 4in (10cm) long taken in late summer. This plant makes a very good hedge.

Lonicera x purpusii

A number of the shrubby honeysuckles are winter-flowering plants grown for their fragrant flowers, which are arranged in pairs and carried individually or in small clusters. These flowers are tubular in shape, opening out to a broad mouth, and are usually white with pale yellow to golden markings. *Lonicera x purpusii* and its parents *L. fragrantissima* (zone 5) and *L. standishii* (zone 6) are some of the best of all the winter-flowering shrubs. They produce frequent flushes of fragrant creamy-white flowers between November and March. The leaves are broadly oval in shape and pale to mid-green in color, carried in pairs on thin twiggy stems. The shrubs often reach 6ft (2m) in height and 10ft (3m) across. These plants will need plenty of room because of their open, spreading habit. ❋ ❋ ❋ ❋ ❋

Propagate by taking hardwood cuttings of nonflowering shoots in winter, or softwood cuttings in midsummer.

RIGHT Lonicera x purpusii *is a shrubby honeysuckle much valued for its flowers in the depths of winter, particularly as they are so heavily scented.*

BELOW RIGHT *The Chinese witch hazel has fragrant, golden yellow flowers. This plant is a first choice for a winter garden.*

BELOW Hamamelis x intermedia *'Hiltingbury' is a distinguished winter-flowering shrub with coppery-red flowers.*

BOTTOM RIGHT Ilex x altaclerensis *'Golden King' tends to produce only a sparse crop of berries and is valued more for foliage than fruit in the winter garden.*

trees and shrubs ✳ 89

Mahonia x media 'Lionel Fortescue'

This is a tough shrub with an upright habit, growing to about 10ft (3m) high. It is ideal for a shaded area of the garden. The glossy, dark-green, leathery leaves are subdivided and made up of many lance-shaped, sharply toothed leaflets. From late fall until early spring, the strongly scented flowers are a rich yellow, carried in dense spikes up to 16in (40cm) long on the shoot tips. A cultivar worth considering for a smaller garden is *M. x m.* 'Winter Sun', which has deep-green leaves and bright yellow flowers, produced in arching spikes on the tips of the shoots. Most mahonias grow best in a moderately fertile soil with plenty of organic matter and free drainage. These plants will often become very leggy and may need severe pruning on occasions—this is best done immediately after flowering has finished, so as not to lose next year's blossoms. ✳ ✳ ✳ ✳ ✳ ✳

Most mahonias prefer to grow in full or partial shade. Prune immediately after flowering by removing the dead flowers.

Parrotia persica

Commonly known as the ironwood, this deciduous tree grows up to 15ft (5m) high and often 30ft (10m) across. It is a close relative of the witch hazel (*Hamamelis*). It has a wide-spreading habit, and is grown mainly for its attractive leaf color in the fall. The leaves are oval in shape with a rounded base and are mid-green in the spring and summer, turning crimson-red and gold in the fall. Tiny crimson flowers with hairlike petals appear in late winter and early spring before the leaves emerge, and the dark-brown bark of mature plants flakes off to reveal pale golden yellow patches, which make patterns on the trunk and branches in the winter. Although often slow to establish, this plant is well worth the wait. There is also a weeping form of this tree, *Parrotia persica* 'Pendula'. ✳ ✳ ✳ ✳ ✳ ✳ ✳

Propagation is by layering softwood cuttings taken in summer or by seed sown in the fall.

Prunus x subhirtella 'Autumnalis Rosea'

This is a spreading, deciduous tree with broadly oval-shaped, dark-green leaves with sharply toothed margins, tinted purple when they emerge in the spring and turning to a dull golden yellow in the fall before they are shed. The tree has an open, spreading crown with slightly lax branches, eventually reaching 25ft (8m) across. The remarkable thing about this tree is that it will hardly stop flowering between late fall and mid-spring. Unless the weather is below freezing, there is rarely a time when the tree does not carry some semi-double rose-pink flowers, although it is rarely totally covered. The flowers fade and open in steady succession. There are weeping forms of this tree as well as one with double pink flowers. ✳ ✳ ✳ ✳ ✳ ✳

These trees thrive in well-drained, fertile, moisture-retentive soil and prefer a sunny position that is not too exposed.

Rubus cockburnianus

Known as the ghost bramble, this is a very thorny, hardy plant that develops long, arching, rich purple-colored shoots that are partly covered with a white waxy bloom, which make this suckering shrub a spectacular feature in a winter garden. The brightly colored stems are produced by pruning the plants very hard each spring just as they come into leaf. If pruned annually, this shrub will grow to a height of up to 4ft (1.2m) and spread to 8ft (2.4m) each year. The deep-green leaves are white on the underside. Sprays of purple flowers are produced in summer. The golden-leaved cultivar *Rubus cockburnianus* 'Golden Vale' is slightly less vigorous, but still needs plenty of room to spread. The golden forms may suffer from leaf scorch in summer if grown in a hot, sunny position. ✳ ✳ ✳ ✳ ✳ ✳

These plants will thrive in most soils, providing they are well drained, but can be very invasive, spreading by both suckers and tip-layering as the shoots touch the soil.

LEFT Mahonia x media 'Lionel Fortescue' puts on an outstanding display in winter of deeply fragrant, golden yellow flowers arranged in spikes.

BELOW Parrotia persica produces tiny red flowers with clusters of short, tufty petals from midwinter onward.

BOTTOM RIGHT Rubus thibetanus 'Silver Fern' is one of the ghost brambles, with a white, waxy coating on the stems.

BOTTOM LEFT Prunus x subhirtella 'Autumnalis Rosea' will start producing its small, delicate-looking flowers in the fall and continue blooming through to spring.

Salix alba subsp. vitellina 'Britzensis'

The willows are a large group of hardy, deciduous trees and shrubs, with thin, narrow, straplike leaves carried on thin, whippy stems. Some have attractive catkin "flowers," with colors ranging from creamy-yellow through to a deep bluish black. Others, such as *Salix alba* var. *vitellina* 'Britzensis', have orange-scarlet twigs that make a stunning display through the winter after the leaves have fallen. In order to maintain this brightly colored bark, the plants should be pruned very hard each spring just as they come into leaf, as it is only the new one-year-old growths that are colorful. If pruned annually, this plant will grow to a height of up to 5ft (1.5m) each year. Willows are resilient, hardy plants that will thrive in most soils, even those that are very wet. ❄ ❄

Propagation is by hardwood cuttings, 8in (20cm) long, taken in the dormant season.

Skimmia japonica 'Rubella'

The skimmias are evergreen, slow-growing, aromatic shrubs with thick, leathery, oval- to strap-shaped foliage that is carried on stocky green stems. The male and female flowers are produced on separate plants in spring, followed by orange-red berries on the female plants that persist throughout the winter. Reaching up to 3ft (1m) in height, *Skimmia japonica* 'Rubella' is a male form, producing 4in (10cm) spikes of red flower buds that develop into white, sweetly scented blooms, and leaves that are aromatic when crushed. During the winter, these bold, glossy green leaves are the perfect contrast to the bare stems of flowering deciduous plants. All skimmias will thrive in filtered sunlight or partial shade and prefer a fertile, well-drained soil. Some cultivars need a slightly acid soil to do well. Skimmias are ideal for inner-city gardening as they are very tolerant of atmospheric pollution. ❄ ❄ ❄ ❄ ❄ ❄

Propagation is by semi-ripe cuttings taken in late summer or early fall.

Viburnum tinus

This attractive evergreen shrub is commonly called the laurustinus and has an upright habit when young. When it reaches about 8ft (2.5m) in height, it becomes round-topped in shape and develops a spreading habit. The smooth, broadly oval, dark-green leaves have paler green undersides and are arranged in pairs along the dark greenish brown stems. Each stem ends in a flat cluster of small, white, slightly fragrant tubular flowers that last throughout the winter months. The flowers are followed by small, black, oval fruits. Possibly the best plants are *Viburnum tinus* 'Eve Price', which has flowers of a deep rose-pink in bud, opening to white flushed with pink, and *V. t.* 'Gwenllian' with dark-pink buds, opening to pale pink flowers. The variegated form *V. t.* 'Variegatum' has cream margins on the leaves. ❄ ❄ ❄ ❄ ❄ ❄ ❄

Propagation is by semi-ripe cuttings taken in early summer. Will grow in a wide range of moderately fertile soils in full sun or partial shade.

Yucca filamentosa

Commonly called Adam's needle, this is a striking evergreen shrub that thrives in poor, sandy conditions, providing the soil drainage is good. The long, straplike leaves are a bluish green in color. The leaf tips form a sharp, spine-like point that usually looks brown and dried. The reddish brown flower spikes grow 5–6ft (1.5–2m) high and are covered with large, white, drooping, bell-shaped, lily-like blooms that are produced over several weeks in early to mid-fall. There are variegated forms of this plant: *Yucca filamentosa* 'Bright Edge' has a narrow golden margin to the leaf edge and *Y. f.* 'Variegata' has creamy-white margins on each leaf. It is possibly the most popular of the cultivars. Unfortunately, the variegated forms tend to be less hardy than the green form. ❄ ❄ ❄ ❄ ❄ ❄

Remove the flower stalk after it blooms or it may collapse over winter and make the plant look untidy. Propagation is by division or rooted suckers removed in spring and planted.

TOP LEFT *Skimmias offer protection to other plants as well as a display of orange-red berries well into winter.*

TOP CENTER Viburnum tinus *is a superb evergreen shrub, producing a succession of pink-tinged flowers. It also offers protection to early-flowering bulbs.*

ABOVE *The orange-scarlet stems of Salix* alba subsp. vitellina *'Britzensis' appear like fire in the garden in winter. Prune severely, as young stems give best color.*

LEFT Yucca glauca *is reasonably hardy, but may need some protection in severe winters.*

trees and shrubs ✳ 93

fruits of
THE SEASON

t often appears at first glance that the time for harvesting and gathering produce is at the end of the year, after which the plant is able to rest before starting again the following year. However, even though fruit-bearing plants growing outdoors have few or no leaves during the winter, and there are no obvious signs of growth, there is still plenty of activity happening inside the plant. These plants will often require a period of chilling (with temperatures lower than 36ºF [2ºC]) to bring about chemical changes within them. This chilling period will influence the quality of blossom produced by the plant in the spring, which is a major factor in determining the eventual fruit crop.

Cultivated fruit trees and bushes (as well as fruiting wild and hedgerow plants) need this period of apparent inactivity for changes to take place within the cells to allow the growth of the buds, which will eventually flower and lead to the new crop of fruit. These were formed during the summer before, while the previous crop of fruits was still developing.

In nature, continuity of the species would be ensured because these fruits would eventually shrivel and fall to the ground. The seeds encased within the fruit would come into contact with the soil as the fruit gradually rotted or was eaten by a bird or an animal. Harvesting the fruit disrupts this natural process, but not necessarily in a beneficial way. The timing of the harvest and the method of handling the fruit will greatly influence its storage life. Harvested fruit that is fully ripe will have a very short storage life and the gas given off by it will serve to accelerate the ripening process of other fruits within the same store. Any damaged fruit will ripen rapidly and start to decay within a very short period of time, possibly infecting surrounding fruits. Even when harvested and sorted correctly, the fruit continues to ripen and will eventually decay, which makes proper storage conditions important to slow down this development to the slowest possible rate.

RIGHT *These homegrown apples have been collected and are ready for storing. Any fruits that were bruised or damaged during harvesting should be used as soon as possible.*

harvesting fruit in winter

Handling is the most important aspect of harvesting fruit, unless it is destined for winemaking. Even a small amount of bruising can affect the rate at which fruit will ripen, and any slight injury will speed up the ripening process and lead to rot setting in around the damage. Once fruit has been picked, it will continue to ripen, so the best methods of storage are those geared toward slowing down the ripening process as much as possible and for as long as possible in order to preserve as much fruit from the harvest as you can.

ABOVE *Orange-red rose hips adorn the arching briars along the country hedgerows in winter. As the weather becomes colder and food harder to find, birds and small mammals will come to rely on these fruits to help them survive through the depths of winter.*

HARVESTING   Following a few simple guidelines will allow best use of the harvest. Any fruit showing signs of bruising or damage should be either used straightaway (if the damage is slight) or discarded (if the damage is severe). Fallen fruit that is sound can be kept, but it is usually in a more advanced stage of ripening (that is why it fell off the parent plant) and these "windfalls" should be used immediately rather than stored.

Unripe fruit should never be stored with ripe fruit, as the presence of ripe fruit will accelerate the ripening of the unripe fruit. Fruit must never be gathered wet. Ideally, it should be gathered early in the morning, while the fruit is still cool.

Some hedgerow plants that have a culinary use need chilling to soften the skin. Sloe (*Prunus spinosa*) can be harvested after the first frost and steeped in a solution of sugar and gin to make the liqueur Sloe gin, and rose hips (*Rosa* spp.) can be boiled into rose-hip syrup (said to be higher in vitamin C than orange juice). Other less commonly grown fruit, such as quince (*Cydonia vulgaris*), also need cold to ripen fully and will store for up to three months. Medlar (*Mespilus germanica*) should be harvested with the first frost and stored until they are overripe before being used.

COMPETITION   As the days and nights become colder, it is more than the weather that will concern the gardener during the late fall and early winter harvests. The local wildlife will show an interest in any edible fruits, because, to them, your fruits are just larger versions of the ones in the hedgerows. Rabbits, mice, and foxes will be happy to forage for fallen fruit, saving you the effort of sorting through the windfalls to see which are worth saving, but some birds fall into a different category. They will peck at fruits that are still ripening on the plant, with grapes being a particular favorite, growing inside under protection or outdoors. The tendency of birds to take a "taste" peck at fruit and then try another is a source of much annoyance to

gardeners as these slight injuries rapidly lead to the onset of fungal infection and rotting. In severe cases, protective nets may need to be used until the fruit is harvested.

STORING FRUIT It is important to create storage conditions that control the temperature, humidity, and atmosphere around the fruit and maintain them at a constant level, as regular fluctuations can speed up the ripening process. If the storeroom becomes too warm, or the levels of certain gases increase, ripening will accelerate and it can be extremely difficult to slow this process down again.

The provision of a good storeroom for fruit can be difficult. A shed, garage, loft, or spare room is often converted into a fruit storeroom, not because it is the best place for the purpose, but because it is the only place that can be spared. Some places are better than others. Storage rooms with wooden floors are less satisfactory, as they tend to become too dry for storing most fruits—buildings with a floor of brick, tiles, concrete, or even earth are better. Whichever the type of storeroom, it must be frost-free and vermin-proof.

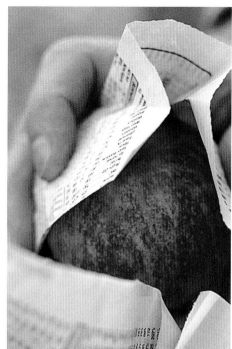

ABOVE LEFT AND ABOVE *To store apples well, it is important that they do not make contact with one another. This means that they should be stored widely spaced, or where space is limited, they should be individually wrapped in wax paper or newspaper.*

The storeroom should be kept dark for as long a period as possible, but provision must be made for ventilation so that whenever necessary the atmosphere in the storeroom may be completely changed. This ventilation is most important because fruit gives off a natural gas (ethylene) as it ripens, and if this gas is allowed to build up, it will accelerate the ripening process, which increases the level of gas, which accelerates the ripening process even more. Whenever there is a strong smell of ripening fruit in the storage area, it is a sign that the gas is building up and the area needs ventilating.

An even temperature of about 39–41°F (4–5°C) through the winter is suitable for most stored fruit, particularly apples and pears. Always store quinces separately, away from other fruit, as they will produce enough gas to ripen surrounding fruits.

BELOW *Some cane fruits with very flexible stems can be trained into loops to save space. These new stems can be trained along support wires during the winter.*

The ideal storeroom should be either fitted with tiers of good sturdy benches or with solid wooden drawers. If this is not possible, find an area where boxes of fruit can be placed, stacked, and easily moved. Where long-keeping fruits are to be stored in boxes, plenty of air space should be allowed between the stacks for adequate ventilation. Long-keeping apples will last better in storerooms if they are first stacked out of doors (but under shelter) in apple boxes or trays for a week, to sweat and allow the fruit surface to dry naturally before going into storage.

Another method of storage is to pile the fruit on the floor in heaps. Large quantities of both apples and pears may be kept in this way, but the heaps should not be more than about 2½ft (75cm) high, or the lower layers of fruit will be damaged by the weight of those above them. For long-term storage,

each fruit should be wrapped in wax paper (or newspaper) to protect the skin and stop the fruit from touching one another to reduce rotting. Fruit can be stored in clear plastic bags to reduce drying out, but no more than 4–6lb (2–3kg) per bag, and the bag should be closed but not sealed.

FREEZING For very long-term storage (often several years) some fruits, especially those intended for use in pies, jams, or desserts, can be deep frozen. While freezing may be an ideal solution with a glut of fruit, the preparation for freezing produce can become very tedious.

INDOOR HARVESTS For generations, gardeners have used greenhouses and conservatories to extend the growing season, and it is possible to harvest edible plants growing indoors when the weather outside is getting severe. Grow plants such as citrus, grapes, and tree tomatoes, also known as tamarillo (*Cyphomandra betacea*), to extend the growing season into winter.

The tamarillo is an ideal plant for the greenhouse or conservatory, especially if it is grown in a container so that the plant can spend the summer months outdoors where the flowers are easily pollinated by bees. Bring the plant indoors before the first frosts, where the bright red, edible fruits will continue to swell and become ripe by midwinter. The same plant can be grown for up to five years, but will eventually become too large to manage indoors. By saving a fully ripened fruit, the seeds can be extracted and sown to produce fresh plants.

Grapes make an excellent choice for a soft-fruit crop in a larger greenhouse or conservatory, but they do need regular attention to ensure a good crop. They are often planted outdoors and trained inside through a hole in the wall to allow the roots plenty of room. 'Black Hamburgh' is the most popular cultivar as it is a reliable cropper and will grow well even in an unheated greenhouse, producing ripe fruit by mid-September. Harvest the bunches of fruit by cutting them off the plant with a short stalk (or "handle") to avoid touching the grapes, and store them in a cool, frost-free, dark place in boxes of straw, where they will keep for up to two months.

Among the most durable fruit-bearing plants for growing indoors are members of the citrus family, with lemons, limes, oranges, kumquats, and tangerines all being suitable for growing indoors and capable of producing fruits when grown in containers, providing these are at least 2ft (60cm) in diameter and 2½ft (75cm) deep. To grow well, these plants prefer a warm,

damp environment, especially when they are flowering, but fruiting can be variable from one season to the next. Citrus fruits will often take about seven months from pollination to ripening, depending on temperature and light level, and in low light conditions the fruit will stay green for a long period, even after reaching their full size. Harvest ripe fruit by cutting them from the plant, leaving a short stalk attached to the fruit. Fruit in good condition can be stored at room temperature for several weeks, although they store just as well by keeping them on the plant until required. This means that there may be ripe fruit, green fruit, and flowers on the plant at the same time.

PROTECTED HARVESTS To advance the crop so that it can be harvested earlier, most fruits are given extra heat. One exception is rhubarb, which is kept cool and dark when being forced for an early spring harvest. The crowns are covered with straw and a waterproof container to block out the light. This hardy plant is technically a vegetable (because the edible part is a leaf stalk) and is one of the easiest early spring foods to force and harvest.

ABOVE *A ripe green quince (Cydonia oblonga) nestles among the gray-green leaves. The fruit is usually ready to harvest in late fall. Judge the ripeness of a quince by its scent; it will still be hard, but when it is very fragrant it is ready to be picked.*

RIGHT *The leaves are long gone, but the ripened fruits hanging from the tree will soon provide a feast for passing birds during the winter. The nearby conservatory makes a comfortable vantage point from which to observe the antics of the birds as they feed.*

LEFT AND FAR LEFT *The stems of rhubarb that we eat are, in fact, leaf stalks, and the plant is really a vegetable and not a fruit. Rhubarb is ideal for forcing to get some fresh homegrown produce during late winter and early spring months.*

storing fruit for winter

As apples and pears mature, an abscission layer develops where the stalk of the fruit is attached to the tree. Eventually, the stalk will separate from the tree at this point and allow the apple to drop. Ideally, harvesting should take place shortly before the apple is ready to fall, at a time when the fruit will separate easily from the tree when it is pulled or twisted gently.

Unfortunately, all of the fruit on one plant does not reach this stage simultaneously, and the choice is whether to pick over the plant several times, or to wait until the majority of the fruit appears ripe and harvest the lot.

For fruit that is intended to be stored for as long as possible, it is better to pick it slightly early, although picking the fruit too early may result in some fruits shriveling in storage and a lack of flavor on ripening.

If fruit is picked too late, it should be used quickly as it will deteriorate rapidly. How carefully the fruits are handled is as important as timing. You want to ensure that they have dry, undamaged skins. Do not leave in direct sunlight after picking, and if picked on a warm fall day, leave in the open (under protection) overnight, then store the fruit early on the following day.

AUTHOR'S TIP:
Storage conditions

Use wooden boxes with raised corners and wide spaces between the slats on the sides and base. This will allow for good air circulation around the fruit, which will help to keep it cool. Do not allow fruits to stand near anything that is likely to taint them. Fresh paint or wood preservatives, for example, can quickly ruin the flavor.

CLOCKWISE FROM TOP LEFT

Pick the fruit from the tree carefully to avoid causing any scratches or bruises, and lay them loose in boxes or seed trays in a cool place overnight to reduce the "field heat" and lower the temperature of the fruit.

Prepare the fruit for storage by carefully inspecting each piece for damage. Reject any bruised fruit. Wipe with a damp cloth to remove any surface dirt and grime (and any fungal spores).

For long-term storage, wrap each piece of fruit in wax paper or newspaper, and place it in a clean, dry tray.

Repeat until the trays are full. The stalk of the fruit should be positioned facing upward, and if there is sufficient room, leave a small space between each fruit.

Place the trays of apples in stacks within the storage box. Always place the fruit to be used first closest to the entrance or on the tops of the stacks (this will avoid having to move all of the boxes to access them).

Check the fruit regularly, and remove any that show signs of rot. Many cultivars of apple and pear will increase in color, with greens taking on a yellow flush, and red and pink colors becoming brighter.

TOOLS FOR THE JOB
Damp cloth
(for wiping the fruit)
Wax paper or newspaper
(for wrapping the fruit)

MATERIALS
Quantity of just-picked
apples or pears
Storage box or chest
Storage trays

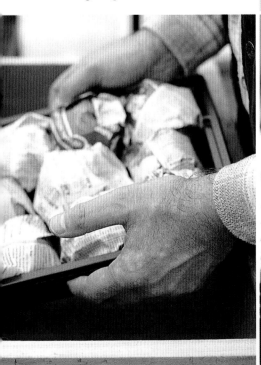

fruit directory
Proper storage conditions are essential to slow down the development of harvested fruit and to prolong its storage life. Careful handling is important to ensure that the gardener will profit from a continuous supply of fruit.

WINTER FRUITS THAT NEED STORAGE OR PROTECTION

FRUIT	DESCRIPTION	HARVESTING AND STORAGE
	**Cydonia oblonga** (Quince) Quince can be used in desserts or for cooking and preserving. They are unsuitable for eating raw as they have a bitter taste and gritty texture. They prefer a warm, sheltered position and are easy to grow, relishing a deep, fertile soil that is moisture-retentive.	The fruits should be left until late fall, when they have turned a golden brown. They will continue ripening when stored in a cool, dry place, and are ready for use from late fall into midwinter.
	**Fortunella** (Kumquat) Kumquats come from China and are among the hardiest members of the citrus family: They can survive temperatures as low as 23°F (-5°C) for short periods. There are two basic types: *Fortunella japonica,* with small, yellow, rounded fruits and *Fortunella marginata,* which has broadly oval-shaped fruits.	The fruits can take up to eight months from pollination to ripening, but this will vary according to temperature and light levels, with plants in cooler, shaded areas being the slowest. Harvest the fruits by cutting them from the plant with scissors or pruning shears. They can be stored for several weeks before they must be used. Both types of fruit are usually eaten unpeeled.
	**Fragaria x ananassa** (Strawberries) These low-growing, fruiting herbaceous plants will grow in most well-drained soils. Fall-fruiting (perpetual) strawberries produce most of their fruit through the late summer and into the fall.	Pick the berries (and their stalks) when about three-quarters of their surface is red. Try to handle the fruit as little as possible as they are very easily bruised. Pick the fruit every other day as they will deteriorate rapidly if left on the plant. Fruits intended for freezing and preserving can be picked slightly earlier than those destined for dessert.
	**Malus sylvestris var. domestica** (Apples) Apples are a popular fruit due to their wide variety of flavors and uses, as well as the long cropping and storing season that runs from late summer to mid-spring, depending on the cultivar. They grow well in most soils, but prefer a deep, well-drained soil. Most cultivars need cross-pollinating in order to produce fruit, so it is important to grow cultivars with flowering periods that overlap.	Late-season apples are picked from mid- to late fall and continue to ripen in storage. They are usually ready for use from midwinter until late spring if stored in good conditions. To test whether or not apples are ready for picking, lift one of the fruits up in the palm of the hand and twist it slightly. If the apple and stalk comes away from the spur easily, it is ready. Apples must be handled with care as they bruise easily, causing them to deteriorate rapidly in storage and encourage surrounding apples to rot.
	**Prunus domestica** (Damsons) Damsons are noted for their sour taste, more suited to cooking or preserving than eating fresh. They tolerate more rain and less sun than plums, although they like similar growing conditions. They flower slightly later, with most cultivars being self-propagating.	Allow the fruits to ripen on the tree. When they are slightly soft to the touch, they are ideal for harvesting as dessert fruit. Those wanted for cooking should be picked while still firm. Harvest from early to mid-fall.
	**Prunus domestica italica** (Greengages) Greengages are a better-flavored form of plum, ideal for eating fresh or bottling, but they tend to average only about two-thirds of the yield of dessert plums. They prefer more sunshine than other plums, and most cultivars are self-propagating.	Allow the fruits to ripen on the tree, and when they are slightly soft to the touch, they are ideal for harvesting as dessert fruit. Those for cooking should be picked while still firm. Ripening greengages are prone to splitting and rotting in wet weather, and attack from birds and wasps in hot weather. Harvest from midsummer to mid-fall.

WINTER FRUITS THAT NEED STORAGE OR PROTECTION

FRUIT	DESCRIPTION	HARVESTING AND STORAGE

Pyrus communis var. *sativa* (Pears)
Pears can be used fresh in desserts or for cooking and preserving. They prefer a warmer climate than most apples, but are almost as easy to grow. They flower earlier and are more susceptible to spring frost damage. Pears prefer a deep, fertile soil that is moisture-retentive, as they are sensitive to drought.

Timing is critical and pears must be picked before they ripen; if left too long, they will rot almost immediately in storage. Mid-season cultivars are picked from early to mid-fall before they are fully ripe. They continue ripening in storage and are ready for use from mid- to late fall. Late-season pears are picked from early winter and continue to ripen in storage. Always use the smallest fruits first. Most forms of pear require moderate pruning in winter to stimulate the next season's growth and fruit, and to maintain an open, well-balanced structure.

Rheum x *cultorum* (Rhubarb)
Rhubarb is a herbaceous perennial, grown for its edible leaf stalks (petioles), which can be used for desserts from early spring onward, making it one of the earliest fresh fruits. Although we treat it as a fruit, technically rhubarb is a vegetable, which is easy to grow and provides the ingredients for many delicious desserts.

Pick the rhubarb when the stalks are about 1ft (30cm) long and deep pink in color. Grip the stalk as close to its base as possible and gently pull it from the crown with a twisting motion. Cut off the leaves, as these are not edible.

Ribes uva-crispi (Gooseberry)
Gooseberries are easy to grow and are reliable crop-bearers. They can be grown individually, as they are self-propagating and do not need a pollinating cultivar. They can be trained against a fence or wall to keep them growing in a confined space. There is a wide range of fruit types, which vary in color from red, yellow, white, or green, depending on the cultivar chosen.

Harvesting times for gooseberries start in midsummer but vary from early, mid-, or late season, depending on the cultivar. Those grown for cooking are picked while still green, but dessert cultivars are allowed to ripen fully before harvest. While the fruit is ripening, some protection against birds may be required. Gooseberries can be frozen and used later.

Rubus idaeus (Raspberry)
Raspberries can be used for fresh desserts, cooking, and jam making, as well as being ideal for freezing. The flowers are self-propagating and lead to delicious fruit, which may vary in color from a blackish red through to golden yellow depending on the cultivar. Fall-fruiting types produce fruit over a six-week period from late August, on the top one-third of the current season's growth.

The berries are fully ripe when they can be picked from the fruit stalk by gripping them gently between finger and thumb. Pull them from the plant, leaving the core or "plug" behind. The fruits must be picked carefully as they are very easily damaged. Fall-fruiting types should be pruned in late winter, before any signs of new growth, when the fruiting canes are cut back to ground level to stimulate the production of new canes.

Vitis vinifera (Grapes)
Grapes can be eaten fresh, processed for juice, stored in a cool, dry place, or used in winemaking. They are one of the oldest of all domesticated fruits. The fruits range from blackish purple, greenish white, or yellow in color, depending on which cultivar they come from.

Cut ripe bunches of grapes with a short section of stalk and place them in a container lined with tissue paper. If not bruised, grapes will keep for up to two months in a cool, dry storage.

winter
FRAGRANCE

Winter-flowering plants are among the most strongly scented of all the plants in our gardens. This is a result of a natural evolutionary process to attract the few pollinators that are around at this time of year. It is essential to the plant's life cycle that flowers are pollinated and fertilized for seed production to take place and to guarantee the survival of the species. The use of scent is very much part of a natural survival process. Species introduced into the garden from the wild tend to have a stronger scent (but smaller flowers) than plants that may be closely related to them but that have been interbred for larger flowers or for a longer flowering period.

Although they originate from a wide range of areas, the different species seem to be trying to outdo one another in the perfume stakes in order to compete with other plants flowering at the same time. This can make it a real delight on a calm, sunny day as a multitude of scents fills the air. Each species attracts pollinators in its own way: Winter-flowering honeysuckles are often described as having honey-scented flowers; the evergreen daphne (*Daphne odora*) has a spicy scent; and *Mahonia japonica* produces a scent similar to that of lily of the valley. Perhaps the best range of scents comes from members of the *Viburnum* genus, with certain species described as having the scent of cloves, jonquil, heliotrope, or even a sweet scent all of their own. Whichever of these appeals to you, there will be more than enough to choose from and enjoy. In fact, it is easy to use too many scented plants, so that the benefits are lost in an overwhelming smell.

Positioning these plants is important in order to get the full benefit of the fragrance. Ideally, some plants, particularly the small ones or those with a more delicate scent, should be placed close to a path or walkway, while the larger or more straggly plants (or those with a very strong scent) would be better placed in the center or at the rear of a border.

RIGHT *Some of the most strongly scented trees and shrubs produce their flowers during the winter months. The wintersweet* (Chimonanthus praecox) *has long-lasting flowers that produce a strong perfume.*

flowers with fragrance

To have no plants flowering in the garden during the winter months would be a wasted opportunity. Flowers opening during the darkest days of winter never fail to lift the spirits. It is always a source of amazement that any plant would expose its most delicate parts to the snow and bitter cold. When accompanied by a heady scent, it is an added bonus that encourages the keen gardener to experiment further. Just realizing the enormous potential of so many plants with such a range of perfumes can be like a voyage of discovery.

LEFT *The sweetly fragrant scent of* Daphne bholua's *pink flowers, produced in winter, is truly outstanding. This plant has a narrow, upright habit and is an ideal choice for a confined space at the back of a border.*

BELOW *Hardy cyclamen are among the finest early-flowering plants in our gardens. These deceptively delicate plants, with their purple, pink, or white blooms, are incredibly hardy and are a perfect choice for growing in dry, shady conditions.*

It would be unwise to give the impression that all winter-flowering plants are heavily scented because some are not. Even worse, some actually have a very pronounced and rather unpleasant smell. One winter-flowering herbaceous perennial, the stinking hellebore (*Helleborus foetidus*), has a less than pleasant scent if the leaves are bruised, while the scent of the spurge laurel (*Daphne laureola*) is described by many as unpleasant and, to make matters worse, the small, greenish flowers are not that noticeable, so the curious are drawn even closer to the plant to see if it is actually blooming.

Although many winter-flowering plants are heavily scented, it is important when designing and planning a winter garden to site the plants so that maximum benefit is gained from what is often a relatively short flowering and even shorter fragrance period. The flowers may only be fragrant during the time when the flower is fully open, so although flowering can last for several weeks from buds opening to flowers fading,

the peak fragrance period may only be about one-third of that time. Another practical problem that may need to be taken into consideration when planning is that many of the scented flowering bulbs are very short stemmed, so the full benefit of their fragrance is difficult to appreciate in a normal garden situation. During late fall and into winter, the sweet scent of *Cyclamen hederifolium* and *Crocus longiflorus*, and later, in midwinter, the fragrance of *Crocus chrysanthus* and *C. laevigatus,* can be missed unless they are planted in large drifts, simply because they are such low growers. If low-growing plants are planted in beds raised about 2ft (60cm) above ground level, the full benefit of their fragrance can be appreciated.

By carefully selecting a range of plants that produce scented flowers through winter, it is possible to achieve a continuity of scents, as well as flowers. This is more realistic than trying to have the maximum number of fragrant plants flowering at the same time, which has its drawbacks. The flowers may look attractive, but too many scented plants close together will spoil the effect as different fragrances compete with one another and the beauty of each fragrance is lost in a cloud of pleasant but indistinguishable scents. Plant several of the same plant, such as *Mahonia x media* 'Lionel Fortescue', which will flower all at once, or in a smaller garden, a mixture of, say, *M. lomariifolia* and *M. japonica*, so that there is continuity of flowering, with *M. japonica* coming into bloom just as *M. lomariifolia* finishes.

Planning and planting

When siting scented winter-flowering trees and shrubs so that the most benefit can be obtained, take their entire habit into consideration. The obvious approach is to site the plants as close to a path or walkway as possible, but unfortunately many of the plants that provide a garden with its winter color often have little to recommend them at other times of the year.

So, it is important to strike a balance when positioning these plants, between being able to smell the flowers without having to trample over the soil and disguising them with other plants during the summer. Some of the taller-growing plants that have a strong perfume, such as wintersweet (*Chimonanthus praecox*), witch hazel (*Hamamelis*), and mahonia, need to be grown farther back in a border because of their size, and in the case of mahonia, its prickly leaves. If they can be grown behind deciduous plants so that they are seen in all of their glory through the winter months, but are partially obscured through the summer months, then so much the better. Do take every aspect into consideration when planting as, for example, *Hamamelis* species also tend to have glorious colors in the fall.

Growing plants close to buildings can be a useful method of gaining the maximum effect of any perfume given off by their flowers, especially when those plants are positioned close to a window or door. Whenever the window or door is opened during the flowering period, even a small amount of the

ABOVE *The most notable of winter-flowering shrubs are the witch hazels, which produce delicately scented blooms.*

ABOVE RIGHT *The deciduous* Viburnum farreri *bears clusters of delicate, scented pink flowers.*

BELOW *The hardy evergreen* Clematis cirrhosa var. balearica *produces large numbers of sweetly scented flowers from late fall until mid-spring.*

scent can be noticed and fully appreciated indoors. Plants grown close to buildings often flower slightly earlier than their counterparts standing farther away in the garden because they benefit from the residual heat being released from the walls. Unfortunately, the disadvantage to this growth being slightly ahead of the season is that when a harder period of cold sets in, these plants are usually the most severe casualties, and a whole season's flowers and fragrance can be lost overnight.

Fragrance does not have to be confined to outdoors, and many scented winter-flowering shrubs can be used as cut flowers, with stems of partly opened flowers brought indoors and placed in water. These flowers will open and gradually envelop the room with a cloud of fragrance, often for a week or more before they need to be replaced. Hyacinth and narcissus bulbs and crocus corms can be "forced" in bowls to flower indoors earlier than they would outside, producing displays of flowers in shades of white, pink, blue, and yellow, which are valued as much for their perfume as their color.

WINTER-FLOWERING FRAGRANT PLANTS

Almond scent
Corylopsis pauciflora

Clove scent
Edgeworthia papyrifera
Viburnum carlesii, V. x juddii

Cowslip scent
Corylopsis spicata, C. wilmottiae

Exotic scent
Eriobotrya japonica

Freesia scent
Mahonia haematocarpa

Fruity scent
Sarcococca ruscifolia

Heliotrope scent
Viburnum fragrans

Honey scent
Lonicera fragrantissima,
L. x purpusii,
L. standishii

Incense scent
Luculia grandifolia, L. standishii

Jasmine scent
Stachyurus chinensis

Jonquil scent
Viburnum foetidum

Lily scent
Osmanthus x fortunei

Lily-of-the-valley scent
Mahonia japonica

Primrose scent
Corylopsis himalayana, C. wilsonii

Soft/sweet scent
Clematis cirrhosa

Soft scent
Eupatorium weinmannianum
Hamamelis japonica
Mahonia repens

Spice scent
Abelia serrata
Daphne odora
Sarcococca saligna

Sweet scent
Abeliophyllum distichum
Arbutus hybrida
Camellia sasanqua
Coronilla glauca
Daphne collina

Dirca palustris
Fothergilla gardenii
Helleborus odorus
Jasminum nudiflorum
Loropetalum chinense
Luculia gratissima, L. pinceana
Mahonia bealei, M. lomariifolia,
M. napaulensis
Sarcococca hookeriana, S. humilis
Spiraea pubescens
Viburnum x bodnantense

Unpleasant scent
Daphne laureola
Helleborus foetidus

Vanilla scent
Abelia chinensis
Forsythia giraldiana, F. ovata
Gordonia alatamaha
Stachyurus praecox

Very sweet scent
Hamamelis mollis

Violet scent
Chimonanthus fragrans
Daphne mezereum

planting a container-grown plant

Using a container is often the ideal way to grow a favorite plant, particularly if the type of soil in the garden is totally unsuitable for it. Any problems that arise tend to happen if the plant grows too tall for the container it was planted in, unbalancing it and causing it to blow over.

The plant may also overbalance if it is very tall because, if a new plant is not supported properly while it is establishing, constant rocking in the wind will prevent its roots growing into the new potting soil around the rootball, and the plant may eventually die. This problem can be overcome by using two short sections of wood or bamboo cane to form a cross that will use the rim of the container to hold the base of the plant firmly in position.

This support will anchor the rootball and enable the roots to develop, while allowing the stem to flex in the wind, helping it to thicken naturally as it grows. The taller the plant, the more important it is to allow the stem to move but to keep the root system stable. This will also reduce the number of times the pot blows over in windy conditions. The cross is hidden just below the level of the potting soil.

AUTHOR'S TIP:
Good drainage

The container should have a sufficient number of drainage holes in the bottom (at least a 1in [2.5cm] diameter hole for every 1ft [30cm] diameter at the base of the container). Rapid drainage is usually much easier to rectify than waterlogging.

CLOCKWISE FROM TOP LEFT

Place a sheet of paper over the drainage holes in the bottom of the container to reduce the amount of soil washed out when it is first watered. Fill the container with potting soil so it is at the correct level to support the plant's rootball (the top of the rootball should be 2–2³⁄₄in [5–7cm] below the rim of the pot).

Remove the plant from its growing container and lower it into in the new container to sit on the soil base.

Add potting soil to about 2–2³⁄₄in (5–7cm) below the rim, spreading it evenly. Shake the container to settle the soil evenly around the rootball.

Make a cross out of two pieces of wood (the arms of the cross being identical in length to the diameter of the rim of the container) and fasten them together with wire.

Wedge the cross horizontally into the sides of the container just level with the soil. Fasten the plant stem to the cross with strong wire.

Cover the cross with potting soil to hide it. Immediately after planting, water the soil thoroughly to settle it around the plant's roots and to remove any air pockets.

TOOLS FOR THE JOB
1 small saw

MATERIALS
1 large container
1 container-grown plant
Sheet of paper
(newspaper is ideal)
Potting soil
2 pieces of wood
(bamboo sticks are ideal)
Wire

planting a rootballed plant

Many plants are sold as "balled-and-burlapped" plants, where a globe-shaped portion of soil is lifted around the plant's roots and the whole lot wrapped in a piece of sacking material (burlap). Such plants can be difficult to handle, as the vibration of moving and transplanting the plant may break open the rootball and harm the roots.

Recently planted trees and shrubs will be able to support themselves as soon as the roots are sufficiently established, but they will require some support initially, especially when planted in exposed positions.

The roots of a balled-and-burlapped shrub or tree will grow into the surrounding soil more quickly if they are not rocking in the planting hole because the crown of the plant is too heavy and shifts dramatically in the wind. You may therefore need to stake or anchor a new plant for the first year or so. Ideally, the support should allow the plant's main stem to flex a little in a breeze, as this process helps to strengthen the trunk. Insert stakes into the ground carefully so that you do not damage the plant's rootball.

AUTHOR'S TIP:
Winter planting

When planting dormant trees and shrubs in winter, apply any fertilizer to the soil surface after planting. The winter rains will wash some of the fertilizer down into the soil close to the roots, so that it is where the plants need it when they start to grow in the spring.

CLOCKWISE FROM TOP LEFT

Mark out the planting hole to about twice the diameter of the rootball, and dig the hole at least twice the depth of the rootball, keeping the topsoil separate from the less fertile subsoil.

Break up the sides and bottom of the hole using a fork. This will allow the new roots to grow into the soil around the planting hole. Add a layer of soil back into the hole and firm it gently.

Place the tree into the center of the hole, and check that the plant is at the correct level—the top of the rootball should be $1\frac{1}{2}$in (4cm) below soil level, or even with the soil level if planting in heavy soil. Untie the root wrapping and gently pull it away from the base of the plant.

Fill the hole with layers of soil, spreading it evenly around the rootball, and firm each layer with a boot heel, until the hole has been filled to its original level.

Drive a support stake into the soil surrounding the planting hole at an angle of 45 degrees toward the tree, and tie the tree to the stake at about 1ft (30cm) above ground level using a strap tie and spacer. Apply a dressing of fertilizer to the surface of the soil.

Mix the dressing lightly into the topsoil around the tree.

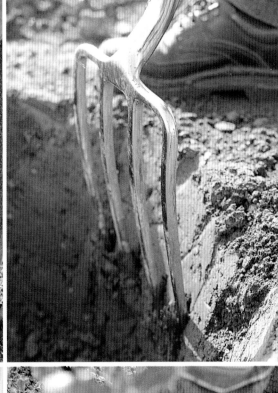

TOOLS FOR THE JOB
1 garden fork
1 garden spade

MATERIALS
1 rootballed plant
Compost
Fertilizer
1 wooden stake
Strap tie and spacer

trees
AND SHRUBS

Ornamental trees are grown for a variety of reasons, and usually represent the longest-lived and most permanent features in the garden. Trees help to form the garden's permanent framework, and can be used as focal points and living sculptures, as well as to define areas of the garden. Particularly in smaller gardens, which can sometimes only accommodate one tree, the choice of which tree to introduce will need careful consideration, as it will affect the atmosphere and appearance of the whole garden.

Garden trees have a range of uses and attractive characteristics. Their size and volume will hide eyesores and provide color and shade, or even provide a support structure for the most vigorous of climbing plants. Many trees will withstand windy conditions and are useful as windbreaks or shelter belts. Many of the trees used for this purpose may not be deemed ornamental, but their most important contribution is to provide protection from strong winds for the less hardy and more ornamental plants within the garden. As well as providing a framework for the garden, these plants provide the conditions that give the garden its own microclimate, increasing the range of plants that can be grown in that particular situation.

Trees used in domestic gardens have been blamed for causing subsidence when planted too close to residential properties. Some trees do indeed draw vast quantities of water from the soil; a mature willow tree, for instance, will take up in excess of 40,000 gallons (182,000 liters) per year. This can cause shrinkage on clay soils, and in turn, may affect house foundations. To make matters worse, cutting down a tree that is suspected of producing subsidence may lead to the soil swelling with the increased water level, causing heave or lift of foundations. It is better to prune the tree regularly to reduce the size than to remove it. Never plant a new tree closer to a property than its ultimate height; red oak (*Quercus rubra*), for example, reaches around 33ft (10m) high, so it should be planted at least at that distance from a building.

RIGHT *The bare branches of trees and shrubs look particularly spectacular in winter after a recent fall of snow.*

trees for the garden

Choosing the right tree is part of planning a garden; another part is choosing the right site. In a garden of any size, the positioning of a tree should be considered as part of the overall design. Trees are crucial elements in the overall pattern of views, sight lines, windbreaks, and screens, as well as paths, borders, and lawns. A little forethought at this stage will save a great deal of redesigning later on.

SITING There is more scope for positioning trees in a large garden than in one where space is restricted. The center of the garden can be an impractical place to put a tree, as it disrupts views, is impossible to plant around without digging up the lawn, and gives the garden a certain regularity, which may not have been the original intention. Offsetting it to the side of the lawn, possibly underplanted with shrubs and bulbs, can hide an eyesore, create informality, and make the viewer want to explore more of the garden.

In a smaller garden, which may only have enough room for a single tree, the most suitable site is often a corner of the garden away from the house. This is especially true in the front garden, providing your neighbor has not already planted a tree on the other side of the fence in that corner. It will afford privacy, shade for a car, or help to delineate a boundary.

A tree can also be used as a focal point along the boundary at the far end of the garden, helping create a formal effect in a small space. A small but angular-shaped garden may have the tree positioned in either the corner of the angle, or in order to hide an awkward shape, it can be positioned at a point where it will help to act as a disguise and draw the eye away.

SOIL The soil in a garden is often taken for granted, but if it is of a specific type, be it limy, acidic, or heavy and poorly drained, this will have a bearing on the type of tree that can be grown. Although the soil can be prepared to create the best possible conditions to encourage the newly planted tree to establish quickly, it has to be remembered that if the soil is totally unsuitable for the type of tree being planted, the tree will not reach its true potential and display the characteristics for which it was originally chosen.

SIZE This has to be a major consideration when choosing trees for the garden. More than any other plant, a tree has the bulk and shape to dominate a garden if it is out of proportion with the overall scale of the design. Likewise, the effect of a tiny tree may be entirely lost in a large garden, where it is swamped by the surrounding plants.

BELOW *Trees do not have to be an approved shape as they can be pruned and trained for specific purposes. Here, a form of willow (Salix alba subsp. vitellina 'Britzensis') is pruned to ensure a regular display of colored shoots.*

Although most gardens are too small to accommodate forest trees such as beech (*Fagus*), oak (*Quercus*), or maple (*Acer*), there are slower-growing and dwarf forms of these same trees that have very attractive ornamental features and are suitable for a wide range of garden shapes and sizes.

FORM The shape (or form) of a tree can be just as important as its ultimate size, certainly in terms of setting a style or mood. Weeping willows are always associated with water features, such as large ponds. Japanese maples (*Acer palmatum*) are ideal for an Oriental-style garden or courtyard where a light canopy casting dappled shade is required. The stag's-horn sumach (*Rhus typhina*), on the other hand, would be more suited to a modern style of garden with decking or areas of gravel. Trees with a broad, weeping habit such as Young's weeping birch (*Betula pendula* 'Youngii') give a soft outline that is useful for softening the rigid lines of nearby buildings. The cone-like or pyramidal shape of Dawyck's beech (*Fagus sylvatica* 'Dawyck') and the pyramidal holly (*Ilex aquifolium* 'Pyramidalis') are ideal as living sculptures.

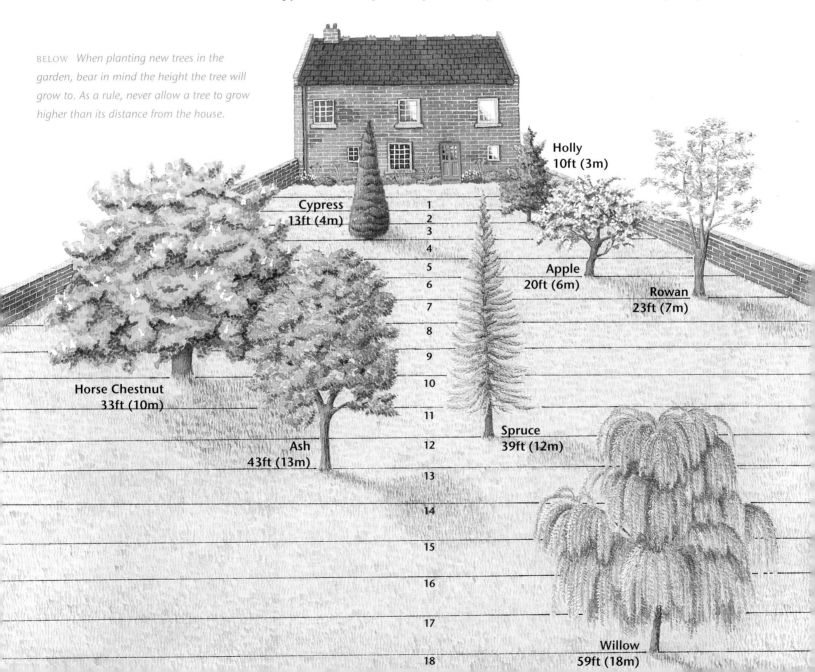

Holly
10ft (3m)

Cypress
13ft (4m)

Apple
20ft (6m)

Rowan
23ft (7m)

Horse Chestnut
33ft (10m)

Spruce
39ft (12m)

Ash
43ft (13m)

Willow
59ft (18m)

1
2
3
4
5
6
7
8
9
10
11
12
13
14
15
16
17
18

Trees are a long-term element in any garden. They are living, growing things that are subject to change—albeit slowly. Not only does their size change, but also their shape. A tree that is catalogued and sold as having a spreading habit may only start to develop in this way as it reaches maturity. One popular ornamental cherry tree, *Prunus* 'Kanzan', has stiffly ascending branches until it reaches 10 to 15 years of age, when it changes to a broader, spreading habit. Many narrow, upright, or "fastigiate" (with branches turning upward) trees will open from the center, allowing the branches to spread out into a broadly conical shape as they age.

PLANTING Where space permits, it is worth considering planting several trees in a group, as a focal point or even a screen. The trees can be planted closer together than the recommended distance of the spread of their crowns, as competition between the trees will produce a combined spreading canopy for the group as a whole.

If space is a problem, consider using a multi-stemmed tree, or a clump planting of several trees of the same species all within a 3ft (1m) square. This will still produce a woodland or tree community, but on a much smaller and more manageable scale than a larger planting. Due to the proximity of the trees to one another, the stems will grow out at acute angles, giving a narrow base to the group but a broad top as the canopy develops. This type of planting looks appealing when trees with attractive bark are used, such as birches, cherries, and maples, which look stunning in winter, especially if winter-flowering bulbs or heathers are planted beneath them.

tree pruning and branch removal

It is important to remove branches from trees and large shrubs in stages, in order to reduce the chance of injury to both the plant and the person doing the pruning. Making a series of cuts to remove the branch in stages rather than all at once provides a degree of control over the removal of the branch.

If this procedure is not followed, and a large or heavy branch is cut flush with the trunk from the top of the branch downward before some of the weight is removed, the results can be disastrous, with the branch tearing down into the trunk of the tree, causing a large, gaping wound that is a potential site for fungal invasion. This type of damage may eventually result in the tree having to be removed completely.

Most woody plants can be pruned in the period between late fall and late spring. The main exceptions are cherries (*Prunus* spp.), which are often pruned in full leaf in order to reduce the risk of fungal infection.

SAFETY TIP:
For high branches that cannot be reached safely, contact a fully qualified tree surgeon, who will have the special equipment required.

AUTHOR'S TIP:
Wound treatments

Wound dressings can interfere with the plant's natural healing process and harbor harmful disease organisms, so their use is no longer common practice. If a dressing is used for aesthetic reasons, spray water-emulsified asphalt as a very thin coating to darken the cut surface.

CLOCKWISE FROM TOP LEFT

Mark points on the branch, using colored labels and thumbtacks as guidelines for the three cuts.

Using a suitable saw, make an undercut about 1ft (30cm) away from the trunk, cutting through up to a quarter of the branch's diameter. If this cut is made too deep into the wood, the weight of the branch will close the cut and jam the saw.

Make a second cut on the top of the branch, 2–2$\frac{7}{8}$in (5–7.5cm) farther along than the first cut.

When the second cut reaches the point where it overlaps the first, the branch will snap along the grain and should fall clear without twisting or tearing the bark on the trunk.

Make the final cut through the base of the stump to remove the last section of the branch. If you cut too close to the tree, you will create a large wound that is vulnerable to pests and diseases. If you leave too long a stub, the dying wood may also harbor damaging pests.

Brush away any loose bark or sawdust from the freshly cut surface and inspect the wood for any signs of splitting or decay. A clean cut will quickly begin to heal over.

TOOLS FOR THE JOB

1 pruning saw (with a blade at least three times longer than the diameter of the branches being cut)

1 sharp knife (to trim rough bark)

1 ground sheet or plastic sheet (to collect the prunings)

1 shredder (to dispose of the prunings)

Plastic plant labels

Thumbtacks (if required)

cutting back to promote growth by pollarding

Pollarding is the technique of cutting tree branches back to the main trunk to encourage new shoots to grow and to keep the tree a manageable size. Trees and shrubs that have colorful new growth to display in winter, such as willow, are good candidates for pollarding as they will add interest to a winder garden; also suitable are those plants that have extra large and attractive foliage in summer.

Most trees and shrubs are cut back regularly during the spring to within around 2–3in (5–8cm) of the main stem, which can be anything up to 6ft (2m) above ground level. Many vigorous shrubs, such as *S. a.* subsp. *vitellina* 'Britzensis' (willow), are pruned in this way to ensure a reliable display of their bright, colorful shoots.

Pollarding is an extremely good method of controlling the growth of a tree within a confined space, where only light shade is required. However, although plants that are pruned back to the main stem often flower on shoots formed the previous season, the flowers are often sacrificed when they are pruned severely by pollarding.

AUTHOR'S TIP:
Be ruthless

Each year, use a saw to remove a number of old branch stubs left from previous years' pruning cuts. This will prevent overcrowding and reduce the chances of pests and diseases invading any old, dead tissue.

CLOCKWISE FROM TOP LEFT

For any type of pruning, it is essential to have good-quality, well-maintained pruning equipment. Knives, saws, and pruning shears may be needed, depending on the size of the plants and branches that are to be pruned.

Start by removing any shoots forming on the main stem below the branches on the top of the tree, using a pair of pruning shears. Work in from one side of the plant to create a clear working area and make the pruning easier.

Remove any shoots that are dead, dying, damaged, or diseased, and any thin, weak growths. Be prepared to use a saw or loppers to cut out any larger pieces of wood if disease is detected.

Cut back the previous season's growths to just above a bud, within 2–3in (5–8cm) of the main framework of branches. If the shoots now appear to be overcrowded, remove every third shoot by cutting it off flush with the main stem.

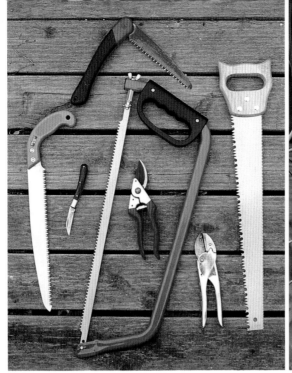

TOOLS FOR THE JOB

Goggles (to protect eyes from flying chips of wood)
Tough gardening gloves
1 folding pruning saw
1 pair of pruning shears
1 pair of loppers
1 wheelbarrow
(to take away the prunings)

MATERIALS

Pruning wound paint (if required)

POLLARDING

Plants with attractive winter stems that can be pruned pollarded include:

Eucalyptus spp. *(gum tree)*

Salix acutifolia (willow)

Salix alba cultivars (willow)

Salix 'Erythroflexuosa'
(orange contorted willow)

Tilia x *euchlora* (green-twigged lime)

Tilia platyphyllos 'Rubra'
(red-twigged lime)

cutting back to promote growth by coppicing

Coppicing is the process of pruning trees or shrubs back close to the ground to encourage strong growth. Ideal candidates for coppicing include woody plants with distinctive stems or colorful bark that will provide an attractive display in winter, or those that produce larger than normal foliage in summer. Unfortunately, the severe pruning of these plants usually means that any flowers that have formed on the previous year's growth will be sacrificed.

Shrubs such as the redtwig dogwood (*Cornus*) are pruned hard to within about 2–3in (5–8cm) of ground level every year to ensure a regular display of their attractive young shoots, which are more striking in winter. Plants such as the golden elder (*Sambucus racemosa* 'Plumosa Aurea') are treated in the same way, although they are grown not for stems but for their large, golden leaves. To avoid a rigid, uniform effect, the height to which these stems are cut can be varied.

COPPICING

Plants with attractive winter stems that can be pruned using this method include:

Acer pensylvanicum
'Erythrocladum'
(pink snake-bark maple)

Cornus alba cultivars (dogwood)

Corylus avellana 'Contorta'
(contorted hazel)

Corylus maxima 'Purpurea'
(purple hazel)

Cotinus coggygria (smoke bush)

Eucalyptus species (gum tree)

Salix alba cultivars (willow)

CLOCKWISE FROM TOP LEFT

Start by taking a close look at the plant and decide which is the best side to start the pruning in order to make working and access easier.

Cut out any shoots that are dead, dying, damaged, or diseased. Cut down into live stems to be sure that all of this troublesome material has been eliminated.

Remove any thin, weak growth to just above a bud within 2–3in (5–8cm) of the main framework of branches. Those plants that are less vigorous, such as redtwig dogwood (*Cornus alba* 'Sibirica'), which is much less vigorous, require severe pruning biennially rather than annually.

All cuts should be made immediately above a pair of buds.

Remove all of the shoots as they are pruned. This will make working much easier and avoids the possibility of pruning the same stem several times.

If the shoots appear to be overcrowded, remove every third shoot by cutting it off flush with the main stem. It may be easier to remove larger sections with a small pruning saw.

TOOLS FOR THE JOB
Tough gardening gloves
1 pair of pruning shears
1 pair of loppers
1 folding pruning saw
1 wheelbarrow
(to take away the prunings)

MATERIALS
Pruning wound paint
(if required)

protecting climbers and wall shrubs

Many plants that are grown against a wall or fence are grown that way because they are only marginally hardy in that particular area and benefit greatly from the protection and warmth offered by the structure. During cold winter periods, additional protection may be required to ensure that these plants come through the winter unharmed, especially if the trees are quite young.

An adjustable cover that can be raised on warm days and lowered for cold spells is the best option. Any insulation material used should allow some light to the plant. This type of shelter should be constructed in early winter, before the worst of the weather sets in. Tender or marginally hardy climbers and wall shrubs such as cherries and the climbing potato (*Solanum crispum*) benefit from this type of protection.

Although the aim is to protect the plant from winter cold, it is important that some light should filter through to it, especially if there are leaves present on the plant, as with some evergreen *Ceanothus* cultivars.

AUTHOR'S TIP:
Winter sunshine

Should the weather turn warm, the protective screen can be rolled up to allow the sun to warm the plant. This will help to prevent the plant's growth from becoming too soft and will discourage any harmful pests and diseases from taking up residence under the shelter.

CLOCKWISE FROM TOP LEFT

Trim the plant to remove bits of damaged growth and tie in any shoots that are loose or rubbing. Fix four brackets into the fence/wall. Place two just above the top of the climber, about 6ft (1.8m) apart, with two more fixed close to the base of the plant, again about 6ft (1.8m) apart.

Cut a length of horticultural fleece to 6ft (1.8m) wide and long enough to cover the full height of the plant, allowing an extra 4in (10cm) at the top and the bottom. Fold over the end 4in (10cm) of the fleece and staple it into position (to form a fold at the top and bottom of the length of fleece).

Thread a 7ft (2.1m) cane through the folds at the top and bottom of the fleece.

Hang one cane between the top brackets and fix in place.

Allow the fleece to drape down in front of the plant before hooking the bottom cane onto the lower pair of brackets.

TOOLS FOR THE JOB
1 pair of pruning shears
1 screwdriver
1 sharp knife
1 pair of scissors
1 stapler and staples

MATERIALS
4 x 2in (5cm) predrilled L-shaped aluminum brackets (or cup hooks)
4 x 2in (5cm) screws
1 x 6½ft (2m) length of horticultural fleece (at least 6½ft [2m] wide)
2 x 7ft (2.1m) long bamboo canes
1 ball of garden string

winter
WILDLIFE

Wild animals play a huge part in the balance of nature: eating insects, distributing seeds, and recycling organic matter. Whether or not wild birds, mammals, and even reptiles live in or visit a garden depends to a great extent upon the gardener's philosophy to both the creatures and the garden. They have to feel that they are welcome and safe, or they will not return.

One of the primary requirements for wildlife is adequate cover. This can be provided as easily in an ornamental garden as in a wild or unkempt garden, although areas that are left undisturbed do tend to hold the most allure. Both wild animals and birds prefer to be able to watch what is happening around them, while remaining unseen by other birds, animals, and humans. This provides the sense of security that will make them consider it safe enough to return. If the conditions are right, the garden will become more than just a feeding site—for some species, it will become a home, using the plants as a habitat for nests and burrows.

The dietary needs of wildlife in the garden can be wide-ranging and varied, but if there is one sure way to encourage birds, insects, mammals, and reptiles, it is a water feature of some kind. This will almost certainly guarantee that they will visit a garden to feed or drink.

However, the selection of plants or features within a garden is only part of the story, and creating the right atmosphere will only produce limited interest from local birds and animals if there are domestic animals who consider the garden their territory. Many wild animals and birds will be deterred from entering the garden, at least in daylight hours and however hungry they are, if they can see the local cat lurking too close for comfort.

The frequent use of certain chemicals will also act as a deterrent. Even if the materials that are used are not toxic, the chemical scent (or taint) left behind by the residue will be unnatural enough to keep these visitors away, as well as killing the insects and mites that they came to feed on.

RIGHT *Brightly colored berries on garden trees and shrubs attract many fruit-eating birds, such as this male blackbird, in winter.*

encouraging wildlife into the garden

Gardeners take great pleasure from the plants they grow, but often, without realizing it, the choices they make when selecting what to grow influence which insects, birds, and mammals will visit the garden. With a little extra planning, it is possible to select both native and ornamental plants that will encourage wildlife to feel at home.

BELOW OPPOSITE *The protective outer cage on this bird feeder allows smaller birds to pass through the bars and feed on nuts held inside their inner cage, while keeping large visitors out.*

BELOW *Ivy (Hedera spp.) seeds are ripe from January onward and are enjoyed by a wide range of birds, such as jays, starlings, thrushes, collared doves, wood pigeons, and members of the jay family. The tough, evergreen leaves also provide excellent winter protection at night.*

Throughout the spring, summer, and fall, food is normally in plentiful supply for most wildlife. It is usually during the winter months that life becomes difficult for them if they are not hibernating. Selecting and growing plants that are a source of food through the winter will encourage birds and mammals to set up home close by, so that they can forage through the garden on a regular basis and come to regard it as part of their territory. However, try to avoid getting drawn into the age-old debate about whether or not the plants that these visitors prefer are native or nonnative species— at the end of the day, the wildlife really do not care. On a cold winter's morning when birds are hungry (and they usually are, as some have to eat as much as six times their own body weight each day just to survive) they will not care if the plant they are feeding on came from England, China, or North America, just as long as the fruits are edible.

At night, they will roost in those trees that provide the best shelter and safety, regardless of whether the plant is an English yew (*Taxus baccata*), an evergreen oak (*Quercus ilex*), which originated in the Mediterranean, or a North American Lawson's cypress (*Chamaecyparis lawsoniana*).

PEST AND DISEASE CONTROL   One of the major benefits of having wildlife visit or reside in the garden is their help with pest and disease control, particularly through the spring and summer months. Slugs, snails, aphids, vine weevil grubs, leatherjackets, and caterpillars will all be gratefully devoured by a wide range of birds. Hedgehogs will happily feed on slugs, snails, and vine weevil grubs (as will frogs and toads) plus whatever insects they can find. There will be times during the season when certain pests may reach epidemic levels and the damage caused becomes unacceptable to the gardener. The wildlife population is unlikely to be able to cope with these high populations and a chemical alternative may need to be used on such occasions. This more organic approach to gardening is a rewarding one, but for many gardeners, it can be a complete change of management philosophy. Chemicals are used only as a last resort rather

ABOVE *Many of the birds that visit our gardens in winter are very agile and will entertain any onlookers for hours with their feeding antics.*

LEFT *When the weather is cold and food is in short supply, there are frequent disputes between visitors over who should feed and who should not. Usually these arguments are brief and quickly forgotten.*

than as a reflex action, and even then they are kept to an absolute minimum, and replaced wherever possible by an organic alternative, such as the use of grapefruit skins to trap slugs.

It is important to keep the wildlife visiting the garden on a regular basis, and one of the better ways is to provide encouragement when conditions are harsh and they are struggling to survive. Providing some food through the winter will entice birds and animals to visit the garden each day and adopt it as part of their territory. Leaving out food scraps or nuts will provide the incentive for these visitors to forage through the whole garden rather than just a feeding area or bird feeder. Birds such as finches, blue tits, and great tits can often be seen clambering over trees and shrubs, pecking at the branches. Usually, they are searching for, and feeding on, the overwintering eggs of aphids or similar insects. A major source of food for larger birds in particular tends to be the seeds, fruits, and berries taken from the plants growing in and around the garden. Planting fruit-bearing trees and shrubs is a long-established ploy used by gardeners to provide color in the winter garden,

encouraging wildlife into the garden ✳ **133**

ABOVE *A gray squirrel feeds on fruits coated in winter frost. These agile and acrobatic visitors will happily steal food that has been left out for birds and small mammals.*

BELOW *This shy young fox may well be a frequent visitor to the garden, but will rarely be seen. Foxes usually prefer to make their house calls after dark, or early in the morning.*

the added bonus being the range of birds and mammals, from the tiny mouse to the much shyer fox, that will eat the same fruits and seeds to supplement their diet.

WATER The inclusion of a water feature in the garden will entice a wide range of amphibians, birds, insects, mammals, and reptiles to drink and feed by the water, with some even needing water in which to reproduce. The most important consideration here is to have at least one point along the rim of the feature where the bank gently slopes into the water, making it accessible to the smaller mammals and birds without the risk of them falling in and drowning.

LIGHTING Committed wildlife gardeners will often extend the range of garden visitors they can watch by installing garden lights, which can be turned on at night, gradually increasing the intensity over a period of time until the aniamls are used to it. This type of lighting enables the viewing of badgers, deer, foxes, and hedgehogs, which all feed at night.

PROBLEM VISITORS Unfortunately, it is not easy to be selective about the wildlife that visits the garden, and there are certain unwelcome guests who may start feeding on the plants that the gardener would much rather keep.

Some members of the finch family are notorious for the damage they can do to fruit trees by eating the dormant buds in the winter, while wood pigeons will quickly demolish any leafy vegetables they can find. Both of these problems can be overcome by draping protective nets over the target plants, but the flight and feeding habits of the birds must be studied to provide the best possible protection. For instance, wood pigeons will walk under net into the vegetable plot, so protective nets must be anchored to the ground so that the intruders cannot walk under them.

Rabbits, deer, and gray squirrels can also cause problems by feeding on plants, and in the case of the squirrels, stealing food that has been left out for birds, and digging up bulbs and herbaceous perennials. In very cold weather, rabbits and hares will gnaw at the bark of trees, especially apples, leaving gaping wounds on the trunk and in extreme cases killing the tree.

ABOVE A birdhouse provides vital cover and protection from wind and snow for birds in winter, or some birds may seek shelter in winter foliage.

LEFT A typical sight in the winter garden— a robin in snow. These little birds are very protective of their territory and will fight off any rivals.

BELOW Many birds, including this starling, will travel miles to find fresh water. This is important as they must have water to help them swallow and digest any food they find.

PLANTS THAT ATTRACT WILDLIFE TO FEED ON THEIR FRUITS IN WINTER IN THE GARDEN

Shrubs
Aucuba (Japanese laurel)
Berberis (Barberry)
Callicarpa (Beauty berry)
Cotoneaster
Hypericum (St.-John's-wort)
Leycesteria formosa (Himalayan honeysuckle)
Ligustrum vulgare (Privet)
Mahonia (Oregon grape)
Pyracantha (Firethorn)
Rosa spp. (Wild rose)
Sambucus spp. (Elderberry)
Skimmia
Symphoricarpos (Snowberry)

Trees
Crataegus spp. (Hawthorn)
Euonymus europaeus (Spindle tree)
Ilex aquifolium (Holly)
Malus spp. (Crab apple)
Prunus padus (Bird cherry)
Sorbus aria (Whitebeam)
Sorbus aucuparia (Mountain ash)
Taxus baccata (Yew)

Climbers
Hedera (Ivy)
Lonicera (Honeysuckle)

making a bird feeder

In order to attract birds and other types of wildlife into the garden, it is necessary to offer a variety of foods and (if possible) a range of feeding sites to meet the needs of the different types of creatures being attracted into the garden. Spreading the food over several sites also makes it possible to feed a large number of creatures at the same time.

The most important times for birds to feed are early in the morning and late afternoon (about one hour before dusk). Wild birds will only normally need supplementary feeding between late fall and early spring, but once feeding has started, it should be continued through the winter, as many species will come to rely on these feeding sessions.

Although there are many manufactured bird feeders available, it is very easy to make one at home with a few simple household items and a recycled plastic bottle.

The following list of foods will attract a wide range of wild birds into the winter garden: baked potato, chopped bacon fat, chopped fruit, cooked rice, cheese, meat bones, fresh coconut, uncooked pastry, mixed nuts, oats and oatmeal, peanuts, raisins and sultanas, stale bread and cake, and sunflower seeds.

AUTHOR'S TIP:
Encouraging birds

The size of the holes cut into the plastic bottle can be used to try to determine which birds will feed at the feeder. Larger holes will encourage larger birds, which can get their heads through the feeding holes. Also, to encourage certain types of birds, stock the feeder with the type of food they prefer.

CLOCKWISE FROM TOP LEFT

Thoroughly wash an empty ½ gallon (2 liter) plastic bottle and remove all of the outer wrappings and labeling. About 4–6in (10–15cm) from the base of the bottle, mark four circles 1¼in (3cm) across at equal distances around the bottle.

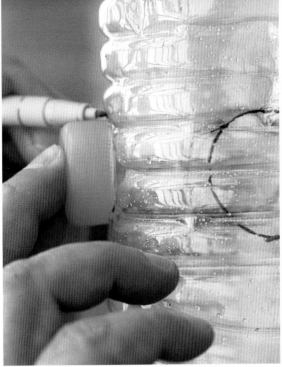

Cut out the four holes in the sides of the bottle (without leaving any sharp jagged bits of plastic). About ½in (1cm) below each of the feeder holes, make a small hole by piercing the plastic with the pointed blade of the scissors.

Cut two 6in (15cm) sections of thin cane or stick with the pruning shears, and push them through one of the small holes and out through the opposite hole, leaving four small perches about 1in (3cm) long protruding from the plastic bottle, each one just below a feeder hole.

Fill the bottom of the bottle with gravel to about ½in (1cm) beneath the perches.

Remove the cap from the bottle, and drill a small hole through it. Thread some string or thin wire through the hole. Refit the cap. Place bird food in the feeder to the level of the bottom of the feeder holes. Hang the feeder in an appropriate place, where the birds can find it and start to feed.

TOOLS FOR THE JOB
1 pen
1 pair of strong sharp scissors
1 pair of pruning shears
1 small hand drill and drill bit
1 pair of wire cutters or pliers

MATERIALS
1 plastic bottle (with cap)
1 thin cane or stick (pencil thickness) 1–1½ft (30–45cm) long
Small quantity of gravel
1 x 2ft (60cm) length of string or thin wire

creating an overwintering shelter *In order*

for wildlife to feel secure in a garden, they must be able to hide. They need somewhere they can sit and observe without being seen. When they feel really safe, they may choose to raise their young in the garden or close by, using the garden as a base and as a source of food and shelter for at least part of the year.

Many small animals will find their way into a garden shed, while frogs and toads will get into a greenhouse, where the moisture levels are much higher. Old pots and boxes, especially if there is straw or paper for warm bedding, will be commandeered by creatures wishing to bed down for the winter. Often the shelter is selected because it has more than one entrance or an escape route, which is why old drainage pipes are so popular.

Wood piles, compost bins, and even piles of garden rubbish that have remained undisturbed for long periods may provide shelter and this can present problems for the gardener. Although burning garden rubbish and prunings is still the best way to dispose of diseased plants and prevent infections spreading, it is a wise precaution always to move the material to the place where it is to be burned at the last moment, or to turn over the heap before lighting it. This way, you can be sure there are no animals hibernating there.

Leaving piles of "clean" clippings or leaves in remote corners will encourage the wildlife to hibernate in areas of the garden where they can be left undisturbed.

AUTHOR'S TIP:
Masking your presence

Always wear gloves while preparing the shelter, as the weaker the human scent around the shelter, the more quickly it is likely to become occupied.

CLOCKWISE FROM TOP LEFT

Start by selecting a wooden box or container that is at least 12 x 12in (30 x 30cm) long and wide and 6–8in (15–20cm) high. This will be large enough for a hedgehog or smaller mammals. Have both ends open if possible.

Place the container in a sheltered, dry position, preferably away from a main footpath in an area that will remain undisturbed all winter. Loosely scatter a few handfuls of dry leaves or straw inside the container.

Start laying stems and branches along the sides of the container, and gradually over the top of the it, until it is hardly visible.

Leave gaps in the top layer of branches so that it will be possible for animals to reach the shelter.

The shelter is more likely to be used if it is well disguised and hidden. Often the only indication that the shelter is occupied will be the occasional rustling noise around dusk as the occupant moves around inside, either to wake up or settle down for the night. The shelter may be given several trial runs before it receives approval as a winter residence.

TOOLS FOR THE JOB
1 small saw
1 pair of pruning shears
1 wheelbarrow
Thick gardening gloves

MATERIALS
Wooden box or similar suitable container (to form the base of the shelter)
Some dry leaves or straw
Mixed prunings and garden waste (dry)

jobs for WINTER

Winter provides an opportunity to carry out many jobs that the busy gardener does not have time to tackle at other times of the year. Repairs, maintenance, construction, cultivation, pruning, and other tasks can all be done in winter, and will often set the tone for how successful the coming gardening year will be.

This is the time to move or propagate dormant plants. Any plants that were not suited to a particular place can be resited or removed, and new ones introduced. Planting in late fall and early winter is beneficial because the soil will still have some of its summer warmth. Often, plants transplanted at this time will develop new roots before going into dormancy for the winter, growing underground even though the top of the plant appears to have shut down for the season.

Many of the more vigorous gardening jobs are undertaken in the winter. This may be for convenience, because it is easier to see what you are doing when there are less leaves on the plants, or for practicality because of the weather. When working outdoors in winter, it is essential to do jobs that make it possible to keep warm, rather than static tasks where intricate finger work is required. This is why so many construction projects are left until the winter months as the work involved generates warmth.

If the weather is too bad to be outdoors, there are always jobs to be done under cover. Plants growing in a sunroom or house will still need some care and attention. Any plants under the protection of a cold frame or greenhouse cannot be ignored, and extra layers of insulation or protection may be needed to guarantee their survival, even if only for short periods when the weather is at its coldest. Even on the days when there are no physical tasks to be undertaken, winter allows the time for reflection and planning, building on last year's strengths, noting which developments and projects were less successful than hoped, and planning for the coming year.

RIGHT *Early morning is lovely to look at, but keep off! With this much frost, it is better to admire the garden from a distance.*

breakdown of tasks
Although a great number of plants growing in the garden are resting through the winter months, the gardener is far from inactive. With a variety of jobs ranging from cultivating the soil and protecting plants from the worst of winter weather to the construction and maintenance of various garden features, winter in the garden is just as busy as any other season of the year.

PLANT PROTECTION If the garden has greenhouses and frames that are used for overwintering plants or to provide an early start in the spring, there will be a certain amount of plant maintenance to be carried out. Constant checks need to be made for the first signs of pests or diseases, which can easily take advantage of the protection offered to their plant hosts. Particular attention should be paid to hygiene and the removal of any plant debris to cut the risk of infection. Picking over the plants to remove any infected plant material is particularly important for those gardeners who are reluctant to use chemical controls.

INDOOR PLANTS Plants that are actively growing, either in a cool or heated greenhouse or indoors in a house or sunroom, will also need some care and attention. This applies particularly to seasonal plants, such as bulbs in bowls, pot-grown chrysanthemums, poinsettias, and the Christmas cactus (*Schlumbergera truncata*). All will need dead flower heads removed, along with any yellowing leaves as they develop, before mold starts to grow. This task is in addition to careful water management to make sure that their flowering and growth is not impaired, either by overwatering or by allowing the plants to become too dry.

Woody indoor plants, such as hibiscus or citrus, have a tendency to produce soft, sappy growth if they are growing in a warm environment with poor winter light levels, and some pruning will almost certainly be required to keep the growth balanced.

As an energy-saving measure, it is well worth considering methods of insulating greenhouses or sunrooms (see pages 154–5) and cold frames with bubble plastic or a similar material. Just reducing any drafts will save considerably on heat loss and plant casualties through the winter.

OUTDOOR PLANTS Outdoors, some plants will need protection (see pages 148–9) if the winter weather turns severe, especially any newcomers that have been planted since the previous winter. However hardy these are, they

BELOW *Adding extra insulation to a greenhouse will reduce cold drafts. Drafts are one of the main causes of premature leaf fall on indoor plants during the winter months.*

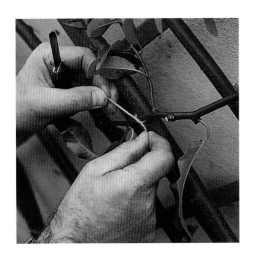

will appreciate some tender loving care to get them through the first winter in a new site. Wind tends to be the real killer, rather than outright extreme cold temperatures. Taller plants, including any plants over 18in (45cm) in height that have not been firmly anchored, and evergreens will be the most vulnerable, or plants growing in containers. Taller plants can be severely damaged by wind rock, where the plant is regularly rocked by the wind and the roots are loosened, or in extreme cases damaged. These plants will need to be re-firmed and staked or protected.

Conifers and broad-leaved evergreens can become victims of wind-chill damage, where freezing winds draw the moisture from leaves faster than it can be replaced by the roots, resulting in brown, desiccated foliage on the windward side of the plant. A temporary screen or shelter can be very effective in preventing this type of damage.

For plants growing in containers, the problem is slightly different, as it is the roots that usually need protection from the cold, either by insulating the container (see pages 160–1) or by temporarily moving the whole plant into a more sheltered environment.

SOIL CARE Basic gardening tasks, such as soil improvement, are a winter job, as there are fewer plants growing and more areas of bare soil between plantings at this time of year. The heavier the soil, the more important it is to carry out basic cultivation, such as digging, in the early fall, not just because the ground conditions are usually drier at this time of year, but because the winter frosts will open up and break down sticky clay soils far better than any cultivation tool so far invented. For heavy soils, the winter frost is far more of an ally than an enemy, and the incorporation of compost or other organic matter will benefit both the soil's structure and the plants growing in it for years to come.

If the soil is not too wet to be structurally damaged by foot traffic and wheelbarrows—or too frozen to dig at all—drainage systems can be installed or improved. Although the summer months are often regarded as the best time for installing drains in a heavy clay soil, the ground can be rock solid at that time of year—as well as occupied by plants.

CONSTRUCTION AND MAINTENANCE Winter gardening is all about one-off projects, as well as routine jobs that are ongoing from season to season and year to year. This is a good time for dealing with construction

ABOVE *Let the weather do the work! Heavy soils can be cultivated and left over winter, so that the frost action will break down any lumps into smaller particles without damaging the soil structure.*

ABOVE *Frozen grass is easily damaged and will die if walked on before it thaws. Problems arise as weeds and moss invade the space.*

LEFT *Newly laid turf may need to be gently firmed several times during mild weather. This tamping will prevent the edges from curling up, causing the grass to dry out and die.*

and landscaping jobs, when sections of the garden may be bare, and it is easy to see the skeleton of the garden layout and make changes for the coming spring.

Repairs and maintenance work often figure prominently during the winter. The lack of vegetation can be a bonus in terms of plants not hindering the work in progress. A good example of this is any water features in the garden, as this is an ideal time not only to drain and clean pools and ponds, but also to do any running repairs to pond sides, walls, and liners (see pages 156–7) while plants are dormant and the fish are lethargic.

The lawn will also benefit from some attention at this time of year, especially during late winter and early spring just before new growth starts. Repairs may consist of releveling (see pages 30–1), changing the shape of a lawn, increasing the shape and size of borders, or reseeding areas where growth is sparse (or places where the grass has died out altogether). The most important fact to remember about the lawn is that no work should be carried out if the grass is frozen. Even footprints made on frozen grass can cause it to turn brown because the cells within the grass leaves are full of ice rather than sap in cold weather. Any contact with the grass will damage the cells, leaving the grass brown and withered once it has thawed out.

ABOVE AND BELOW *Ponds will need extra care and attention during the winter months. Do not allow the surface to freeze over completely for more than four or five days at a time as this may be harmful to fish. Long periods of freezing and thawing may also damage the pond lining.*

pruning and training indoor plants

Indoor plants require regular training and pruning to retain vigor, promote flowering, and control growth. Most plants grown indoors have a longer growing season than their outdoor counterparts and can from time to time look off-color. They may need regular pruning on a "little and often" basis.

Many plants grow more rapidly indoors, which may lead to the plant shedding leaves, particularly on the bottom one-third, which can only be solved with regular pruning and training. The basic principles of pruning and training under cover are much the same as for outdoors, although it might be necessary to adapt them to accommodate the extended growing period and restricted space. Some plants flower only on the new season's growth, and on these plants the old growth may be safely cut back in the spring without harming the production of next season's flowers. Others flower on older wood and should be cut back only after flowering.

The best time for pruning depends on the plant's flowering season, whether the plant produces flowers on new or old wood and the desired purpose of pruning.

AUTHOR'S TIP:
Restricting growth

Remove overvigorous plants from the container, prune the roots, and repot them in the same-sized container. This will reduce the amount of shoot growth because it forces the plant into using a great deal of energy to heal the cut roots and redevelop a full root system.

CLOCKWISE FROM TOP LEFT

With some plants that have become overcrowded, the best method of pruning them may be to divide up the plant completely. Start by removing the plant from its pot.

Divide the plant into sections by gently drawing the separate stems of the plant apart, taking care to minimize any damage done to leaves, shoots, and roots.

Carefully examine the roots of these small, new plants, trimming away any that are obviously bruised or broken.

Repot the new, young plants into small pots and water them thoroughly after placing them in a suitable environment.

With other types of indoor plants, some may only need the tangled stems thinning out by using pruning shears to prune away the oldest and weakest, or any showing obvious signs of pests and disease.

Remove any dead flowers as they begin to fade, and discard them immediately. Leaving such dead tissue lying around will provide sites where fungal rots, such as gray mold (botrytis) can establish and spread to colonize live, healthy plants.

TOOLS FOR THE JOB
1 pair of pruning shears
1 sharp knife
1 bucket or tray
(for rubbish)
Watering can

MATERIALS
Potting soil
Plant pots
Garden twine
(if required)
Seed trays
(or carrying trays for the newly potted plants)

making a temporary plant shelter

Plants can be protected by building a temporary shelter around them as a method of reducing wind-chill damage. Bamboo canes are ideal for use as structural support as they have a degree of flexibility and will bend in high winds rather than break or blow over. Use plastic netting or hessian sacking (burlap) as a cladding to cover the canes as these materials will filter the wind rather than resist it, and will also gather snow or sleet, providing even more protection.

Where possible, leave one side of the structure open to help keep the plant hardy and to allow in some sunlight. The side that is left open should be the most sheltered side of the structure; this side can be closed during periods of bad weather.

Ideally, this type of temporary plant shelter should be constructed in early winter, before the most severe weather sets in. Newly planted conifers and broad-leaved evergreens, such as Elaeagnus, will benefit greatly from this type of protection. This temporary shelter is easy to remove in spring.

AUTHOR'S TIP:
Plastic film

Avoid using plastic film as protection. If the film touches the plants, condensation will form at the points of contact, which will freeze in cold weather, damaging the plant tissue. Plastic film will also allow the warmth inside the wigwam to reradiate out into the atmosphere, often resulting in the temperature being several degrees lower inside the structure.

CLOCKWISE FROM TOP LEFT

Select four 5ft (1.5m) bamboo canes and position each one about 1ft (30cm) from the base of the plant. Push the base of each cane into the soil to a depth of about 6in (15cm).

If the ground is hard, use a hammer to knock the cane into the soil. Once the cane has penetrated the ground, continue pushing it in by hand.

Draw the tops of the four bamboo canes together by bending them gently toward the center above the plant.

Tie the canes together with garden string to form a wigwam frame around the plant, without actually touching it.

Cover three sides of the wigwam with plastic netting or fiber cladding, tying it to the canes with twist ties or string. On exposed sites, bury the base of the cladding in the soil to give extra stability.

Leave the fourth (most sheltered side) open to allow light in. If weather conditions become very severe, pack some loose straw or hay between the plant and the inside of the cladding, and then close the fourth section of the wigwam in order to provide additional protection.

TOOLS FOR THE JOB
1 sharp knife
1 lump hammer
1 pair of scissors

MATERIALS
4 x 5ft (1.5m) long bamboo canes
1 x 16½ft (5m) length of plastic mesh netting, hessian sacking (burlap), or horticultural fleece (at least 6ft [2m] wide)
1 ball of garden string
About 12 wire "twist ties"
Quantity of straw or hay

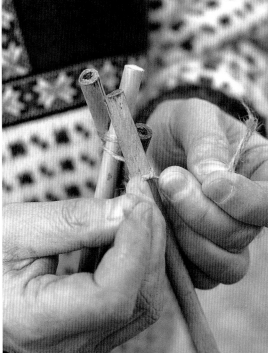

constructing a compost bin
Composted plant material and general organic garden waste is one the most valuable materials that a gardener can use to improve soil. Use compost as either a soil conditioner or a mulch. Either way, it has a very beneficial effect on the garden soil, adding healthy living organisms and improving the soil's tilth or texture.

Possibly the most valuable effect of composted organic waste is the improvement in soil fertility, which results when organic acids are released as the organic matter continues to decompose after it has been applied to the soil. The presence of these acids helps release plant nutrients, which may be locked in the soil and beyond the reach of the plants roots. The incorporation of nutrients into the soil and continued decomposition is largely brought about by soil-borne organisms, such as bacteria, beetles and worms.

Added to a heavy clay soil, compost will help "open up" the soil (allowing more air to enter) and will improve the soil texture, making the soil more workable. In a poor, free-draining, sandy soil, added organic matter will increase the soil's water-holding capacity.

AUTHOR'S TIP:
Extra lining

Lining the bin with black plastic will keep the contents warm toward the outside, as the plastic will absorb the sun's heat, and it will also prevent the compost from getting too dry close to the edges. This is a useful way of making sure that the contents of the bin have an even moisture level and temperature, so it does not have to be turned as often.

CLOCKWISE FROM TOP LEFT

Mark out an area of up to 10sq ft (1sq m) and level the ground with a garden fork or rake.

Using a post driver or sledge hammer, knock in a 5ft (1.5m) post, which is at least 4in (10cm) thick, at the four corners of the area. Leave about 3f (1m) of the post above ground level.

On three sides of the area, erect a 3ft (1m) high fence of $^3/_4$–$1^1/_4$in (2–3cm) mesh wire, and fasten the wire to the outside of three of the posts with staples to make a three-sided bay.

Place the remaining wire mesh on the floor of the bay (to deter rats and other vermin), and fold any surplus up the sides of the bay so that there is an overlap of at least 6in (15cm).

Line the three walls of the bin with heavy-duty black plastic that has plenty of ventilation holes in it. Secure the black plastic to the posts with staples.

Slot a couple of timber boards just inside the two front corner posts to make the final (front) wall of the bay. Add more boards as the compost bin is filled with garden waste. The pressure of the waste pushing against these boards will hold them in place against the front posts.

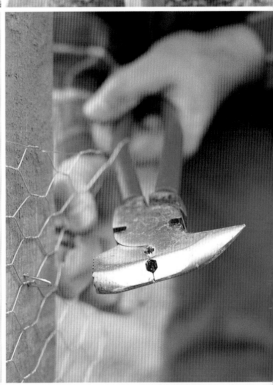

TOOLS FOR THE JOB
1 garden fork or rake

1 sledge hammer or post driver

1 claw hammer

1 pair of pliers or wire cutters

1 garden line

1 staple gun

MATERIALS
4 x 5ft (1.5m) posts, 4in (10cm) thick

Chicken wire (or similar): 1in (2–3cm) mesh, 3ft (1m) wide and 15ft (5m) long

Black plastic sheet 3ft (1m) wide and 10ft (3m) long

1 box of heavy-duty galvanized staples

4 timber boards (cut to size)

drainage systems in clay soil

Heavy clay soils can hold large amounts of water, making digging and other cultivation impossible at certain times of the year. Some form of drainage system will be necessary to lower the water level, so that the upper layers of soil, at least, are drier. The siting and laying of drains in the garden is normally a fairly straightforward procedure.

Drainage systems are commonly arranged in a herringbone pattern, with trenches of about 2–2½ft (60–75cm) deep and 13–16½ft (4–5m) apart on the heaviest clay soils. The floor of the trench should slope gently and evenly toward the lowest point in the garden, with the branch drains linking into the main drain. A layer of ash, sand, or gravel is laid over the top of pipes before the trench is refilled with soil. This porous, vertical layer will act to intercept the water as it moves laterally in the soil and direct it down toward the pipes.

If there is a natural outlet, such as a ditch or stream, the main drain is usually fed into this, but in the event of no obvious outlet, it may be necessary to construct a dry well (see page 31).

AUTHOR'S TIP:
Easy digging

For easier working, lay the drainage system when the soil is dry. If you are working in wet weather, use broad wooden planks to walk on in order to prevent the soil from becoming even more wet and sticky from being trodden on. Dig the trench on a sloping site, starting from the lowest point and working upward so that any water is draining away from you as you work.

CLOCKWISE FROM TOP LEFT

Using a garden line and canes, mark out the route of the drain where the drainage pipes are to be laid.

Dig a trench about 2–2½ft (60–75cm) deep and about 1ft (30cm) wide. Keep the topsoil and the subsoil separate.

Place a 2in (5cm) layer of gravel, ash, or sand in the bottom of the trench, and lay or "bed" the drainage pipes on top of this layer. Place the pipes so that they are touching one another end to end.

Refill the trench with a layer of gravel, ash, or sand over the pipes to within about 10–12in (25–30cm) of the surface.

Fill the trench with topsoil, leaving a slight mound over the trench (this will settle down within four weeks). Do not press the soil into the trench, especially if it is wet.

Spread any remaining soil over the site. It will be incorporated into the topsoil within few months. The drain should feed into an outlet, such as a ditch or stream.

TOOLS FOR THE JOB
1 garden spade or trenching spade
1 shovel
1 wheelbarrow
1 garden line

MATERIALS
Sufficient gravel, ash, or sand to refill the trench
Clay or plastic drainage pipes
2 long, broad, wooden planks

greenhouse insulation

Use insulation in order to reduce heating costs while still keeping the greenhouse warm through the winter. This will reduce drafts and keep warm air trapped inside the greenhouse, close to the plants. If you add a false ceiling inside the greenhouse, that also will reduce the loss of heat through the greenhouse roof (often there are no plants growing in this space anyway).

To get the most benefit, install extra greenhouse insulation in late fall, when much of the sun's residual heat can be trapped within the greenhouse. Plants such as tender geraniums, osteospermums, and fuchsias that are being overwintered in the greenhouse will survive better with this added protection.

The warm, still air within the greenhouse may increase the risk of fungal diseases as well as plant-damaging insects and other pests, so try to ventilate the greenhouse for a few hours when the weather is mild (ensure that the ventilators are covered separately so that they can be opened easily). Use thumbtacks to attach plastic bubble wrap to a wooden frame; for aluminum greenhouses, use small plastic clips, which can be removed in the spring.

AUTHOR'S TIP:
Greenhouse maintenance
Before insulating the greenhouse, refit any sheets of glass that have slipped, and replace any broken sheets of glass with new ones. In fact, this is the ideal time for carrying out minor structural repairs to the greenhouse.

CLOCKWISE FROM TOP LEFT

Start by cleaning the outside glass of the greenhouse, using a soft-bristled brush and detergent or soap and water. Clean glass will allow maximum light to enter through the dark winter months.

Rinse the detergent off the glass with plenty of clean water.

Brush down the support structure inside the greenhouse to remove any debris and overwintering pests and diseases. Then clean and rinse the inside of the greenhouse as before.

Fasten sheets of bubble wrap or clear plastic film to the support structure inside the greenhouse with thumbtacks or clips, leaving an air cavity between the glass and the insulation.

Cut plastic plant labels into thirds, and trap them against the bubble wrap as it is pinned in place. This will apply extra pressure and reduce the chance of the insulation material tearing away from the thumbtack.

Either insulate the roof in the same way, or stretch sheets of bubble wrap or clear plastic film across the inside of the roof to form a false ceiling, which will reduce the chance of heat loss from warm air rising through the greenhouse roof.

TOOLS FOR THE JOB
One 2 gallon (10 liter) bucket
1 soft-bristled brush
1 sharp knife
1 pair of scissors

MATERIALS
Half a cup of detergent/soap
Quantity of clear plastic bubble wrap
(6½ft [2m] wide)
2 boxes of thumbtacks
with large heads (or small plastic clips
for an aluminum greenhouse)
Quantity of 4in (10cm)
long plastic plant labels
(each one will be cut into thirds)

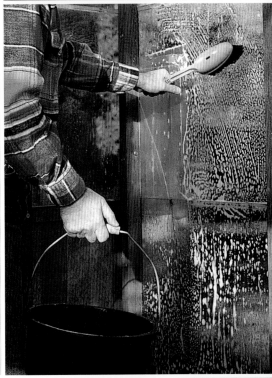

pond maintenance

During summer, when the weather is hot and dry, ponds often suffer a drop in the water level over a period of time, and although this can be quite worrying, it is normal to lose ³/₄–1¹/₄in (2–3cm) of water in a week. However, if the level drops sharply and always falls to the same point after refilling, it is time to start looking for a leak. If water is removed, a wet patch may well form on the lining as water seeps back into the pond from the wet soil on the outside of the leak. This is the simplest way of finding out exactly where the leak is.

Although it may not show until the height of summer, most of the damage caused to the pond will happen in the frosty conditions of winter. The most difficult time to try to repair a leaking pond is after a period of rain when the soil is very wet, as it becomes very difficult to detect the leak.

Most nonflexible pond liners are made of concrete, and most leaks are caused by deep cracks developing within the concrete—usually caused by severe frost or uneven settlement of the pond. The water level of the pond will need to be lowered so that the suspect area can be inspected, and it may be necessary to remove any fish and plants from the pond first.

AUTHOR'S TIP:
Frost damage

Frost is the most common cause of leaks—as water freezes, it expands and the pressure may cause concrete to crack. Leave a block of wood or a plastic ball to float on the surface to prevent a sheet of ice from forming and to reduce frost damage.

CLOCKWISE FROM TOP LEFT

Brush away any dirt or debris around the cracked or damaged area and allow the surface to dry.

With a hammer and masonry chisel, chop out some of the concrete around the crack to make it wider. This will help the sealant to get a good grip and bind into the liner.

Clean the prepared area by brushing out any loose dirt and other debris.

Force waterproof mastic cement into the crack, covering all of the prepared area.

Using a pointing trowel, pack the mastic cement tightly into the damaged area, leaving a smooth surface that is flush with the surrounding lining.

The pond can be refilled the following day, when the cement is fully dry. After refilling the pond, monitor the water level closely for a few weeks to make sure that the leak has been repaired. If the water continues to drop below the desired level, look for wet patches above the water line, as this may indicate fresh leaks where water is seeping back into the pond.

TOOLS FOR THE JOB
1 hard-bristled brush
or scrubbing brush
1 hammer and masonry chisel
1 pointing trowel
1 hose

MATERIALS
1 tube of waterproof
mastic cement

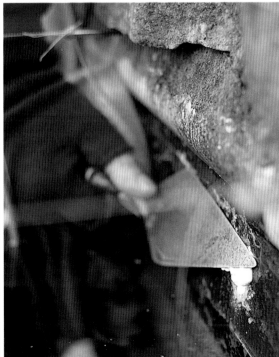

lawn repairs

The lawn is usually the largest and most dominant feature in the average garden, and its upkeep will be one of the major gardening tasks throughout the year. Even the most beautiful lawn will eventually need some surgery, either as a result of wear and tear, accidental damage, or through natural causes. Without realizing we are doing so, we often tend to walk over the same route in and around the garden, sometimes using paths, other times not, creating paths referred to as desire line—a good indicator of where to lay a new path if you are considering it.

Occasionally, part of a lawn edge may become broken or damaged, either when mowing the lawn or when working on one of the other more general tasks as part of maintaining a border.

If this area is left untended, the lawn edge on either side of it will start to crumble and the area will increase in size. The main problem with this type of damage is that a very thin section of the lawn is affected and it can be difficult to try to use the small existing bits of damaged turf for the repair. These small sections, if they are worth saving, will be quite unstable and prone to drying out or frost damage.

AUTHOR'S TIP
Level lawns

Always leave the new piece of turf fractionally higher than the level of the rest of the lawn, as it will soon settle slightly and match in with the surrounding lawn. Within six weeks it should be impossible to spot the area that has been repaired.

CLOCKWISE FROM TOP LEFT

Clean away any crushed or broken sections of turf to make it easier to assess the full extent of the damage and the work involved in repairing it.

Using a half-moon cutter (edging iron), cut three lines into the lawn to form a rectangle that includes the broken edge. Use a wooden board as a guide, to ensure that the lines are straight.

Using a spade or turfing iron, cut horizontally under the turf at a depth of about 2in (5cm) to sever the roots, enabling the turf to be lifted up (cut into the turf from the border and under the lawn, to cause less damage to the lawn).

Lift up the section of cut turf and turn it around so that the damaged section is on the inside of the lawn and the newly cut straight side forms the outer edge. After replacing the turf, firm it gently until it is slightly higher than the surrounding lawn.

Fill the small hole in the lawn (what was the broken edge) with finely sieved garden soil and cover it with a layer of sandy top dressing or garden soil.

Sprinkle a small quantity of grass seed over the bare soil. If kept moist it will quickly germinate and grow.

TOOLS FOR THE JOB
1 half-moon cutter (edging iron)
1 wheelbarrow
1 spade or turfing iron
1 garden fork

MATERIALS
Quantity of topsoil
1 long plank of wood
(with straight edges)
Fertilizer
Grass seed

protecting container-grown plants

All plants have a temperature range within which they will thrive and another temperature range that they will tolerate. Hardy plants that grow outdoors in containers will generally do well in a range of temperatures, but they will grow even better if kept within their preferred range.

The roots of plants are much more sensitive to frost damage and low temperatures than the top growth, mainly because they are usually insulated by a large volume of garden soil. This is why, in a hard winter, plants growing in the soil will survive, while those growing in containers are often killed or severely damaged, as the relatively small volume of soil in the container offers very little protection to the roots. In order to help hardy container-grown plants survive in winter, they need to be moved indoors or provided with some form of extra insulation.

This method of plant protection should only be required when hardy plants are likely to be subjected to temperatures down to 23ºF (-5ºC) for periods of five to seven days or longer. For longer periods of sustained cold, plants should be housed under protection with the insulation removed.

AUTHOR'S TIP:
Sunny days

On warm winter days, lower the plastic cover from around the plant pot for a few hours to allow the pot to absorb the sun's heat. Re-cover it before the temperature drops in order to trap the heat around the plant.

CLOCKWISE FROM TOP LEFT

Place the container-grown plant inside a large plastic bag and fold the top of the bag into the rim of the container. Open a second large plastic bag and put a thick layer of waste paper (old newspapers are ideal for this) in the bottom.

Place the wrapped plant inside the second plastic bag on top of the paper, leaving the second bag open.

Crush sheets of dry newspaper into balls and place them in the space between the two plastic bags, filling the space between the two bags until the balls of crushed paper are level with the top of the plant container. This layer of paper will insulate the plant's roots against low temperatures in winter. Straw can be used for the same purpose; however, any type of insulation material used must be kept dry.

Draw up the outer plastic bag and tie the top into position so that the sides of the container are covered with balls of paper. Take care not to trap any of the plant's leaves in the bag.

The plant may now be left outdoors during the winter season. Remove layers of insulation in spring when the weather starts to get warmer.

TOOLS FOR THE JOB
1 sharp knife

MATERIALS
1 container-grown plant

2 large plastic bags
(garbage bags or similar)

Large quantity of
old newspapers (or straw)

1 ball of garden string

cleaning stems
Many trees and shrubs are grown for their decorative stems and twigs. The paper-bark maple (Acer griseum) or paper birch (Betula papyrifera) have a peeling bark, which always looks colorful as a new layer of bark is exposed each year. Others, such as the silver birch (Betula pendula) and snake-bark maple (Acer pensylvanicum), retain their attractive bark for several years.

After a few years, the bark of trees that do not exfoliate may become dull and discolored. Where the trees are shaded by their neighbors, this will occur naturally as lichens and algae form on the stem, while in more populated areas, pollution and atmospheric dust can cause stem discoloration. When this happens, the attractive bark is not shown off to best effect.

In order to get the maximum benefit from these plants, it is worth considering washing and cleaning the trunks now and again to remove the dirt and grime and to improve the ornamental value of the plant. Washing can also have other benefits, as the scrubbing will dislodge fungal spores and insect eggs that may be overwintering in cracks in the tree trunk. The soap will help dissolve the protective waxy coating on insect eggs, which are then destroyed by drying out in the wind or killed by frost.

AUTHOR'S TIP:
Saving time

If the plant is only to be viewed from one side, then consider cleaning just this side of the trunk, especially if it is a large plant where cleaning the whole trunk would possibly be too great an undertaking.

CLOCKWISE FROM TOP LEFT

On a dry day, throw a bucket of cold water over the trunk of the tree, or pour water over the trunk to soften and loosen the deposits on the bark.

Add one tablespoon of soft soap to a 2 gallon (10 liter) bucket of hot (not boiling) water, and mix it thoroughly into the water. Using a stiff-bristled brush, apply the soapy solution to the tree trunk, starting from the top and working downward, scrubbing vigorously over the surface of the trunk.

Once the area to be cleaned has been scrubbed, and most of the soapy water has drained down to the base of the trunk, reapply the mixture of soapy water to any areas that are still dirty and scrub for a second time. Wash away any residue with cold water.

For trees with a relatively smooth bark, such as *Prunus serrula*, the trunk color can be enhanced by washing it with cold water. A light scrubbing with a soft brush may be necessary in areas with a lot of atmospheric pollution, such as dust or dirt.

After the washed trunk has dried, gently buff the washed areas with a thick cloth.

The finished section will then glisten in the winter sun.

TOOLS FOR THE JOB
1 tablespoon
1 scrubbing or stiff-bristled brush
One 2 gallon (10 liter) bucket
or watering can
1 soft cloth

MATERIALS
Hot and cold water
Small quantity of soft soap

seasonal
RETREAT

One of the best things about winter for the keen gardener is that there is always something to do. Although outdoor plants may not need much attention, there will usually be a selection of plants in the house, greenhouse, or sunroom that need tending on a regular basis.

Indoor gardening can be one of the major preoccupations through the winter, with a range of seasonal display to produce for the Christmas period that can be enjoyed when it is too cold to venture outside. Growing plants indoors is simply an extension of the garden, but without some of the heavier work. It is an opportunity to increase the range of plants grown, and it does involve some skills and techniques that may not be required outdoors.

It is also a chance to become involved with plants even if you do not have a garden at all. As long as you have a window sill, or can put a table near a window to allow the plants enough light to survive, you will be able to produce something colorful. Even forcing a few bulbs in a darkened room or cupboard can give anyone interested in gardening an amazing degree of satisfaction, and may well lead to an increase in interest in other plants. There is an indoor plant for any situation except deep shade, and a little research will yield a wonderful display.

There are other ways for the gardener to work indoors in winter. Work areas, such as the potting shed, need a thorough winter clean (rather than a spring clean, as there are too many other gardening tasks to be carried out once spring arrives) to get rid of any lingering pests and diseases. Greenhouses and other growing structures, such as a cold frame or cloche, that are not in use can be cleaned and sterilized for the coming seasons, and any used border soil or compost replaced or replenished. These are essential good-practice operations, which need to be done regularly for hygiene reasons. Referred to as the "bad weather" tasks, they should be saved for those periods when working outdoors is either impractical or impossible.

RIGHT *Growing a range of houseplants can help to keep the keen gardener occupied during the short winter days.*

winter indoors

Indoor plants have been increasing in popularity since Victorian times. They allow us contact with nature, refresh the atmosphere, and give a room character and color. Most of the plants we grow indoors originated as outdoor plants in warmer countries, with many being tropical or subtropical, and as such they need care and attention to maintain their ideal growing conditions.

ABOVE OPPOSITE *Orchids are very popular indoor plants and their long-lasting flowers make them ideal for growing in the house or sunroom.*

BELOW OPPOSITE *This attractive and varied array of houseplants inside a sunroom will help any garden enthusiast forget about the poor gardening weather outside.*

BELOW *The amaryllis is a seasonal indoor plant that is closely associated with Christmas. With a little care and attention, the bulbs will survive for a number of years.*

These plants would not naturally choose to live indoors, where the air is dry, supplies of water are limited, the growing area is restricted, and the levels of natural light are reduced (and often of poor quality in terms of the plant's needs), especially through the winter months. Even those plants growing inside the house on a permanent basis, which appear to be happy with their present location, may benefit from a change of position within the house as the winter approaches, particularly if they have been in a dark corner. Some plants require a period of dormancy and will need to be moved into a cooler room, such as a spare bedroom or porch area, to allow them time to rest and get ready for the new growing season. Others that normally live on the window sill will have to be brought into the main room, or at least moved into the center of the room overnight, to escape the cold temperatures.

The good thing about winter is that houseplants have less competition for care and attention. Most gardeners spend more time indoors at this time of year and there are quite a number of plants that can be grown "out of season" to bring color into the house. Some are long-term plants, which can be grown for many years and will flower over the winter period, including the Christmas cactus (*Schlumbergera* spp.) and Flaming Katy (*Kalanchoe blossfeldiana*). Others are much more instant, and short-term, but still provide a beautiful display, and may survive and come back to flower for a second time, such as the African violet (*Saintpaulia* spp.). Some plants such as the Panama orange (x *Citrofortunella microcarpa*), the Christmas cherry (*Solanum pseudocapsicum*), and the ornamental pepper (*Capsicum annuum*) are grown for their brightly colored fruits, which can provide color for several months if kept in reasonably humid conditions by standing their pots on a tray of moist gravel. Other seasonal plants include cyclamen (*Cyclamen persicum*), azalea (*Rhododendron indicum*), and poinsettia (*Euphorbia pulcherrima*), which has insignificant flowers and large colorful leaves (bracts) at the end of each shoot.

The range of begonias grown indoors is huge, with some, such as *Begonia* x *elatior*, grown for their wide range of attractive flowers, and others for their colorful leaves (and perhaps flowers as an added bonus), including the

painted-leaf begonia (*Begonia rex*) and the iron-cross begonia (*Begonia masoniana*), both of which have attractive leaf markings.

There are a number of bulbs that can be used for indoor displays, giving color and scent in the early months of the year when there is little else around and many of the Christmas-flowering plants are finishing. Prepared and grown in cool, dark conditions, hyacinths have spikes of heavily scented flowers lasting for several weeks, and for something really dramatic, try amaryllis (*Hippeastrum*) with its tall stem and large trumpet-shaped flowers.

Cultivating plants under protection, whether in a greenhouse, conservatory, cloche, or frame, is usually done to increase the range of plants that can be grown, to provide protection for plants that are only marginally hardy, or to extend the plants' natural growing season.

ABOVE *Cyclamen make reliable houseplants and are easy to care for. Many types have attractively marked foliage, which makes them interesting even after the flowers have faded.*

ABOVE *Cinerarias are attractive, seasonal houseplants that are easy to care for. The small, daisy-like flowers are available in a range of vibrant colors.*

BELOW *Primulas are versatile plants that can last for several years. Some varieties grow indoors, some outdoors, and some do both.*

As a result, any gardener who uses protection in this way has to cope with the fact that there are regularly two seasons on the go at once: the natural season for the locality (outdoors) and an extended or advanced season indoors where plants are growing to slightly different rules, due to the protection they are receiving. This can mean that midwinter outdoors is actually late winter or early spring indoors under protection and so planning and preparation have to begin earlier, as do propagation and growing.

Due to the nature of this protected, and to some extent, controlled environment, the seasons tend to merge into one another. While this maintains a constant period of interest, it can also lead to some very specific problems that can be difficult to overcome. The protection offered to the plants is often taken advantage of by a whole range of pests and diseases, and the extended season and warmer temperatures, coupled with a lack of natural predators, means that many of these problems not only multiply at a faster rate indoors, but also do so for most of the year.

As the growth rate of plants and the multiplication rate of the pests and diseases is at its slowest rate during the winter months, this is usually the best time of year to try to eradicate these problems before the new growing season starts. Tasks such as the fumigation of greenhouses and sunrooms are often carried out in late fall and early winter to eliminate insect pests and fungal pathogens before the new plants for the coming year are introduced. Washing down glass and the supporting structures can be very beneficial at this time of year. Not only does it help the plants during the winter but often for the rest of the year. Where plants are growing under protection in border soil, ideally the soil should be replaced every third year to prevent a buildup of soil-borne pests and diseases, especially if the same plants, such as cucumbers or tomatoes, are grown in the same place every year.

Other, more mundane but equally important indoor jobs, such as cleaning used pots and seed trays, are often saved for this time of year when the weather is too chilly or wet to make working out in the garden a sensible prospect. Sterilizing canes and other plant supports to kill off overwintering insect eggs and fungal spores may appear trivial but is an important preemptive strike toward preventing problems in the spring, and reduces the need to rely so heavily on chemical controls.

Servicing the lawn mower and repairing tools are important tasks that can be carried out in the potting shed or greenhouse when the soil is too wet or frozen to work on or the weather is too cold. The time spent on these jobs now will save time, money, and chemicals later in the year.

ABOVE Gardenia augusta *is a shrubby indoor plant that can produce flowers in winter.*

BELOW *Not all houseplants are ornamental; edible plants or herbs are functional as well.*

making a cold frame

A cold frame enables gardeners who do not have the room for a greenhouse to do some greenhouse gardening on a small scale. Cold frames protect plants over the winter months, including chrysanthemums, geraniums, osteospermums, and many others that need protection from the coldest winter weather in order to survive.

Seeds and cuttings can be started into growth three to four weeks earlier than if they were growing outside in the open. The frame will also keep the air humid around the tops of cuttings and prevent them from drying out. Some gardeners prefer to construct their own cold frame, either from timber with a soil base or a brick-built

frame with a concrete base and wooden lid with glass panels. These structures are excellent for protecting plants, but they are usually fixtures, and unless the frame is correctly sited, they can have limitations, such as lack of light at certain times of the year.

An alternative is to get a self-assembly "kit frame," available from most gardening and home centers. Most are made with materials that have good insulation properties while still allowing good light transmission, and are light and easy to move about the garden, giving the gardener greater flexibility.

AUTHOR'S TIP:
Garden safety

Many of the modern frames are made from polycarbonate materials, which are much more durable than glass. These materials make the frames much less of a safety hazard in gardens where children play, as there is far less chance of them being injured than if glass was used and accidentally broken.

CLOCKWISE FROM TOP LEFT

Remove the contents from the package and check that all the items listed on the assembly instructions sheet are present.

Using the corner clips provided, fit the grooved aluminum edges to the two lid sections (with the hinged bars at one end of each panel). Following the assembly instructions, fit the grooved aluminum edges to the top and bottom of each of the base panels (with the hinge bar on the top of the rear panel).

Next, fasten the corner brackets onto the side base panels. Make sure that they are fixed firmly into position before sliding the front and rear base panels into the corner brackets and fastening them into position using screws.

Attach the lid to the frame's base by sliding the two hinge grooves together on the frame's rear panel. Repeat with the second section of lid so that the frame is complete.

Fasten a spacing bar onto the lid of the frame (this is to allow the frame to be ventilated in gradual stages). Place the frame in its allotted position and add plants that need protection or shelter.

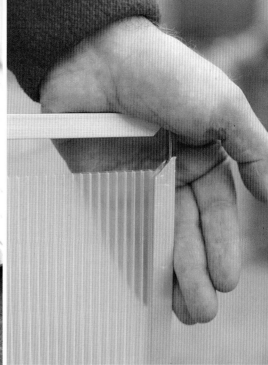

TOOLS FOR THE JOB
1 screwdriver

MATERIALS
1 self-assembly pack for a cold frame, consisting of:
Plastic side panels
Plastic lid panels
Plastic front/back panels
Grooved aluminum edges
Hinge bar fitting (for back of frame)
Hinge bar fitting (for lid sections)
Spacing bar (for ventilation)
Sprung metal corner clips
Self-tapping screws

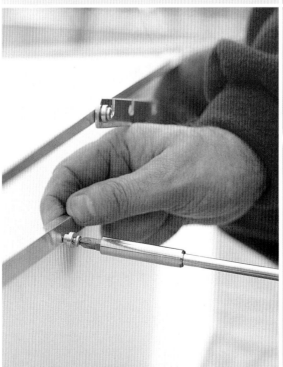

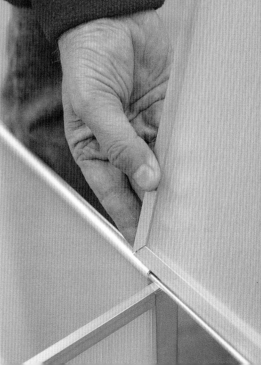

moving container-grown plants

Plants in containers do not need to be regarded as fixtures. If the plants and containers are not too large, they can be moved around the patio or the garden so that seasonal interest can be maintained. Move plants coming into flower into a prominent position and place those past their best out of the way until they recover and start to flower again.

Larger plants can be used as windbreaks or screens and moved according to the prevailing wind. This mobility makes it easier to grow tender plants, as they can be moved under protection when cold weather is forecast and brought back into the open when milder conditions return. Many plants grown in a greenhouse or sunroom will

benefit from spending some time outdoors in the summer, or even a couple of hours in a sheltered spot on a warm day in winter.

For larger containers and plants, it is useful to have the container mounted on casters or small wheels to make moving them about easier. Even if the area is split-level, by laying boards over the steps, it is possible to wheel the container into just about any position. The only limiting factor is likely to be the size of the plant.

AUTHOR'S TIPS:
Variations

Soak the base of terra-cotta pots in a tray of water before drilling. This will make the pot easier to drill into and will reduce the amount of dust that is created if the baked clay is dry.

For square containers, use four wheels or casters, one positioned at each corner of the pot; where circular containers are used, place three casters spaced at equal distances around the base of the pot.

CLOCKWISE FROM TOP LEFT

Select a suitable container, either plastic or terra cotta. Check for any flaws or cracks that may lead to it splitting or breaking. Select three or four suitable wheels or casters. Use heavy-duty ones if the pot is large and the contents likely to be heavy (these will usually have a separate outer metal sheath).

Using an electric drill, make four holes in the bottom of the container. For terra-cotta pots, use a masonry drill (the drill diameter should match the diameter of the outer metal casing of the casters).

Separate the caster from its outer casing and insert the casing into the drilled hole in the base of the pot, from the outside, using a hammer if necessary. For containers with a thin base, use a block of wood with a hole drilled in it (same size as the diameter of the outer metal casing of the casters). This can be fitted over the outer casing of the caster to make it stable and reduce the chance of the container cracking.

Insert the caster into the casing and push it firmly into place.

For a large container, you may need to drill extra drainage holes.

When all the casters have been fitted, turn the pot upright and fill it with the new plant.

TOOLS FOR THE JOB
1 electric drill
(masonry drill for terra-cotta pots)
1 hammer

MATERIALS
1 plant container
3 or 4 wheels/casters
(with attachments)

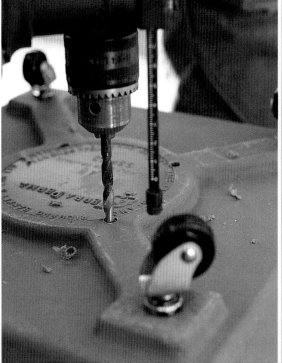

plant
ASSOCIATION

Perhaps the greatest challenge to any gardener is to choose and grow a selection of plants that will complement a theme or aim within the garden. Having a wide range of plants to choose from is all very well, but narrowing down the choice and selecting those plants that not only grow well together, but also work as a community, is one of the more interesting and challenging aspects of gardening.

As the average garden becomes smaller, there is a tendency to select climbing plants to make better use of walls and fences, or where possible, to choose multipurpose plants that will provide interest for as long as possible. The witch hazel (*Hamamelis* spp.) not only provides winter color and fragrance, but its cultivars will also provide excellent fall color, as their leaves change through greens, yellows, and oranges before being shed.

When thinking of blending plants, take all their attributes into account. Do not limit yourself to the colors of leaves and flowers, or the texture of the leaves, but think about stimulating other senses by using sound and scent. Grasses, for instance, provide a gentle background noise as the wind rustles flowers and leaves. Scent is a major factor in any garden, but particularly so in winter as a large proportion of winter-flowering plants are very fragrant.

Aim to blend plants together in harmony in the garden, rather than have any one type or group dominating the remainder. Spread winter interest throughout the garden, if possible, so that the whole garden is worth investigating, rather than concentrating it in one area that will be briefly spectacular, but may be quite dull during the other three seasons. Positioning plants can be particularly important if a subject has a limited period of interest. This type of plant will need to be in a prominent place when it is at its peak of display, but can be almost obscured for the remaining seasons. A selection of both deciduous and evergreen plants can be used to disguise or complement each other as they reach their peak in turn.

RIGHT *Try to select plants that prefer the same type of soil or growing conditions to encourage them to grow to their full potential.*

planting for effect

The whole concept of gardening is to take plants out of their natural environment and arrange them in a managed setting, whether it is formal or informal. The art is to make it appear that the whole effect has happened quite naturally, rather than looking too contrived. Mixing and blending a range of trees, shrubs, bulbs, and herbaceous perennials in a way that appears natural can give any gardener a feeling of satisfaction, especially as the garden matures.

OPPOSITE *Many hardy cyclamen will grow much better in the partially shaded conditions and drier soils found around the base of plants, such as this Japanese maple.*

BELOW *Many birches are fairly shallow-rooted trees that are happy to grow close to water. Here, the reflection of the colored stems on the water enhances the thoughtful planting scheme.*

Some plant combinations and associations will spring to mind as you consider your design. This may be as a result of plantings you have observed when visiting other gardens, or ideas gleaned from books and magazines. The white, pinkish white, or rusty brown stems of birch trees (*Betula* spp.) make a spectacular focal point within any garden, particularly when underplanted with heaths and heathers or hardy cyclamen to provide color and seasonal interest during the winter, when the tree stems are far more noticeable due to the lack of leaves. The very fact that the low-growing plants around the base of the trees may be in full flower or have foliage colors other than green will serve to complement the trees, rather than detract from them simply because their stems are not hidden in any way by these plants.

Plants with colored stems need positioning so that they have a plain (preferably dark) background to act as a foil to show off their colors. Walls, fences, or evergreens will all form suitable backdrops. Plants such as the green-stemmed osier dogwood (*Cornus stolonifera* 'Flaviramea'), or the ghost brambles (*Rubus cockburnianus* and *R. thibetanus*) benefit from this arrangement, as their delicate pale green and white shades are easily lost if the appropriate background is not chosen.

Other combinations may seem less obvious, especially for the winter garden. This is where plants are hidden or disguised to account for a lack of interest at other times of the year or to meet the demand of the plant's natural habitat. Many of the bulbs and corms that flower over the winter period like fairly dry conditions and may resent root disturbance. They also tend to prefer cool, shaded conditions at the time of year when they are dormant, but plenty of light when they are actively growing. The best way to meet these growing conditions and to get a good display from plants such as snowdrops (*Galanthus* spp.) and cyclamen (*Cyclamen hederifolium* and *C. coum*), among others, is to grow them under deciduous trees. That way, they get the light they need in the spring, before the trees have leaves, and they also receive the summer shade they require, when the tree's canopy

blocks the light from the soil in which they are growing. Getting plant association right does mean doing a little research, but it will more than repay the work every year as the plants produce a spectacular display of color.

In some respects, it is much easier to say what will not work in the garden than what will, because ultimately the choice of plants is up to the gardener.

SOIL TYPE AND pH Plants thrive in their ideal soil, perform reasonably in a soil that does not quite meet their requirements, but struggle and die in a soil that is unsuited to them. Limiting factors for grouping plants together are soil type, as most plants have preferences for moisture content and drainage, and the pH (the level of alkalinity or acidity in the soil). Soil type varies widely, even within a small geographical area, depending upon the underlying rock, or where the soil was imported from if the house is new. In a limestone area, the soil is likely to be alkaline, whereas in a woodland area (particularly if there are pines) it is likely to be acidic. You can find out your soil's pH with a testing kit from a local garden center. Acid-lovers are fussy and simply will not survive in a soil with a high pH. Winter- and early spring-flowering plants with a preference for acid soil include witch hazel (*Hamamelis* spp.), camellias, heathers, and *Rhododendron praecox*.

ABOVE *This* Hamamelis x intermedia *has been planted in a spot that catches the low winter sun, making the flowers glow with color to form an attractive winter display.*

HARDINESS Climate will also have a major bearing on how well plants grow, and although plants may be grown in close association to enable the tougher plants to shelter and support the more delicate ones, ultimately their hardiness (or tenderness) will determine a plant's ability to survive in a particular situation. This is even more relevant in a garden that is planted for winter bloom. A particularly cold snap can damage flowers that were encouraged to open during a warm spell. A deciduous plant such as *Daphne bholua* var. *glacialis* 'Gurkha' will benefit from the shelter of large-leaved evergreens or conifers around it to protect it from cold winds and help absorb frost.

With careful planning, both deciduous plants and evergreens (whether they are coniferous or broad-leaved) can be used to provide just enough shelter to increase the range of plants being grown in a garden, by offering protection for those plants that would not survive in a more exposed position. In a smaller garden, fencing, screens, and movable windbreaks will serve the same purpose and provide support for climbing plants.

ABOVE *Here, the hardy* Garrya elliptica *with its catkinlike flowers provides extra shelter for* Iris unguicularis. *The added protection will encourage plants to flower slightly earlier.*

SCENT Combining scented plants to form an association that works may be more difficult, because as well as avoiding clashes of flower color, it is just as important to avoid clashes of fragrance, or the benefit of the perfume from both plants may be lost. Surrounding the scented plants with broad-leaved evergreens or conifers will amplify the intensity of the fragrance and can be used to concentrate it in a certain direction.

Where several species or cultivars of witch hazel are to be used within the same garden, it is far better to select plants that flower at different times to have a continuation of flower color and fragrance rather than having them all out at once. Choose cultivars of the Virginian witch hazel (*Hamamelis virginiana*) to flower in late fall and early winter, hybrids of *H.* x *intermedia* for the middle of the winter period, and cultivars of the Chinese witch hazel (*H. mollis*) for late winter and early spring.

By carefully selecting different species and cultivars of winter-flowering bulbs, such as crocus and snowdrop, it will be possible to have a carpet of blooms opening beneath the witch hazels as they finish flowering. They can also be underplanted with low-growing, winter-flowering plants such as heathers or *Daphne mezereum*.

LEFT *Conifers and heathers are often planted together. Combining plants that come into their own at different times of the year ensures that there will always be areas of interest.*

RIGHT *Crocus chrysanthus 'Princess Beatrix' naturalizing in a grass area is an example of how two different plants with different growth cycles can accommodate one another.*

LEFT *This is a quiet, sunny retreat for the resting gardener. A position such as this is the perfect spot for siting a selection of scented, winter-flowering plants.*

RIGHT *The attractive bark of a prunus and the constant search for extra space from this Hedera helix 'Glacier' have combined to enhance the characteristics of both plants.*

BELOW *A group of mixed grasses catch the winter sun. The yellows and browns of these dead plants can lift the dullness of winter and provide activity as they sway in the wind.*

POSITIONING Within reason, plants that flower during the winter need to be positioned where they can easily be seen and the fragrance enjoyed. They can be planted beside a path or patio, or beneath a south-facing window that is likely to be opened on a warm day so that the fragrance can drift indoors, bringing a welcome reminder that winter does not last forever.

Low-growing plants may not be so easy to smell. One way around this problem is to group several together in a raised bed, perhaps near a seating area, so that they are on a level with a seated person. Bulbs can be planted in containers and kept near the house while they are flowering or dotted in the border among other plants. Once they have finished flowering and begun to die down, they can be removed from the containers and planted in the garden ready to flower again the following year.

Some winter-flowering shrubs have a powerful fragrance, which can be slightly overwhelming in too great a quantity—*Daphne bholua* 'Jacqueline Postill' is such an example. It is a plain shrub for most of the year, but has a blaze of glory during the winter months when its flowers give off a rich, heady fragrance that can be concentrated on a warm, still day into a scent

strong enough to travel across the garden. If you like the scent, this will be a delight, but if not, it may be that the plant would be better placed farther from the house, path, or patio. This plant works well in a border among evergreen shrubs whose leaves will help display the attractive flowers.

TEXTURE The shape and form of the plants in a garden give it texture, and during the winter months this is a feature that exists despite a lack of color. Frost on leaves accentuates their shape and can highlight small details that might otherwise be missed. By mixing evergreens with deciduous plants, shrubs with grasses, and herbaceous plants with ground cover, as well as using bulbs throughout, you will be able to give the garden interest and vitality, which will save it from looking dull in any season.

The sharply toothed leaves of the herbaceous *Helleborus argutifolius* stand out in winter as much as (if not more than) the green flowers, and it will draw the eye to nearby plants. Take advantage of this by planting it at the base of a deciduous *Viburnum* x *bodnantense* 'Dawn', with its pretty pink flowers and delicious scent, and then add a cluster of *Narcissus* 'Jetfire' as a spring bonus. Smaller plants with spiky leaves, such as *Iris reticulata* and the many ornamental grasses, look attractive in front of evergreens with large, rounded leaves, such as *Viburnum tinus* with its heads of pinkish white flowers and blue-black berries. Follow the theme through by planting crocus thickly in a drift, so that their long, thin leaves add to the overall effect.

BELOW RIGHT *Texture does not have to be limited to plants. A combination of hard materials such as pots and pebbles can act to complement the shapes and colors of plants.*

BELOW *The glistening stems of* Rubus cockburnianus *appear to be frozen, but the attractive white color helps to protect the young stems as they are developing.*

Frost also enhances the sharply pointed leaves of *Sarcococca hookeriana* var. *digyna*, which has tiny, fragrant white flowers, and *Ruscus aculeatus*, with its unusual red berries borne directly on the "leaves" (they are actually modified shoots). Plant low-growing bulbs around the edges of the bush for added color, or team with a pink-flowering hellebore, which will stand out all the more for having the foliage to set it off.

Where a shrub is being grown for its attractive stems or contorted branches, such as the corkscrew hazel (*Corylus avellana* 'Contorta'), which looks wonderful against a blue winter sky, the bare stems and yellow catkins blend well with varieties of narcissus. Plant the narcissus for a succession of flowering until the bush is in leaf; for an extended season of interest, plant snowdrops to flower before the narcissus.

There are varieties of bulbs that will flower from January onward through late winter and early spring, and by selecting the right ones, your garden need never look gray at this time. Grow enough and you will be able to cut them for indoors, too. Bulbs will grow in any well-drained soil and can be chosen to complement the other plants in the garden, whether they are in flower or not. Yellow is a cheerful color, and crocus, aconites, and narcissus

blend well with all shades of green, so keep them in full view of the house windows, in front of plain evergreens. White snowdrops and crocus lift a dark corner or a bare deciduous shrub, and where herbaceous perennials have died down, purple crocus will cover the bare soil and give a welcome splash of color until the perennials regrow.

VEGETABLES Plant association is not limited to outdoor or ornamental plants; vegetables have been grown in groups for better management for years. Vegetable groupings are established on the basis of their botanical relationship, because their nutritional and growing requirements are very similar, and because they often play host to the same pests and diseases.

Growing these groups of plants together, but on a different plot of land each year, greatly benefits the plants in the long term (see the crop rotation chart on page 41). Using crop rotation in the vegetable garden will reduce the need to use pesticides and give the land time to recover the nutrients removed by each group.

INDOOR PLANTS Whichever way your window or sunroom faces, there will be a plant to suit the light levels; although during the winter, as the levels fall, they may need moving to make the most of the light that is available. In order to get the best from both plant and situation, it is worth researching several varieties that can grow together and create their own microclimate. This will increase the humidity around the plants and keep them healthy. By mixing foliage plants with flowering or berrying plants, you will show the colors to their best advantage.

ABOVE *The waving golden yellow seed heads of the cardoon (Cynara cardunculus) are silhouetted against the crisp blue winter sky.*

LEFT *The tangled branches of this corkscrew hazel (Corylus avellana 'Contorta') will attract attention before the delicate flowers come out.*

BELOW *The flowering times of hardy cyclamen and snowdrops overlap to ensure a steady supply of changing colors.*

BELOW RIGHT *The low-growing Narcissus cyclamineus is a good choice for naturalizing in a woodland or meadow.*

sap
RISE

Plants can be at their most vulnerable as winter draws to a close and spring brings the earliest signs of a new growing season. In the depths of winter, plants are able to cope with low air temperatures and cold and wet soil simply because they were conditioned to it during the fall; they also have stocks of food reserves to help them cope with weather conditions that are unsuitable for active growth. As days get warmer and nights shorter, growth will gradually begin: undetectable cellular activity at first, followed by the gradual emergence of leaves and flowers, which are often quite delicate.

The varied weather conditions of early spring regularly cause far greater damage than a hard winter. For many plants, the start of a new growing season is marked by chemical changes that happen within the plant, a process triggered as days get longer, although the rate of growth will be determined by air and soil temperatures. Soil temperatures will rise gradually, but constantly, with many plants needing soil temperatures of around 40–45°F (5–7°C) before root growth will commence. Air temperatures, on the other hand, will fluctuate over a 24-hour period and could range from 25–32°F (-4–0°C) at night up to 53–58°F (12–15°C) by midafternoon for many weeks into the new season. This means that plants are subjected to a stop-start growth pattern, with frost damage frequently checking the earliest growth. Even the oak (Quercus spp.), for all its resilience and longevity, can be burned by late frosts, with seedlings only marginally hardier than a houseplant for the first few weeks after germination.

This can be a stressful time for gardeners, tending plants to toughen them up and keep them actively growing, as well as watching the weather for any hints of a snap frost, which can leave carefully made plans for the seasons ahead in disarray. Always have a contingency plan ready, in case plants need to be nursed through the last few weeks of winter and early spring.

RIGHT *Spring-flowering bulbs, such as this* Puschkinia scilloides *var.* libanotica, *indicate that winter is drawing to a close.*

preparing for spring

A wide variety of plants have adaptations that make them capable of flowering in winter. Some, such as Prunus x subhirtella *'Autumnalis', start flowering in the fall and continue through the winter months as long as weather conditions allow. During this time, only flowers are produced; the growth of shoots and leaves is restricted by the low temperatures. Most of the plants growing in a temperate climate are not able to grow actively until the temperature rises above 43°F (6°C), and no amount of coaxing will work until the soil is warm enough for the plants to grow.*

Even if the late winter and early spring days are warm and sunny, air temperature is only one of several factors to influence growth, so that a week of warm sunshine may have little immediate effect on plant growth. The temperature in the soil around the roots, which is usually just above or below freezing, has the most bearing on how early plants start into active growth. Until the soil becomes warmer, consistently over 40–43°F (5–6°C), very little root growth will occur. If the roots are unable to grow, there will be very little top growth on the stems. The soil is generally at its coldest during the early months of the year and will slowly become warmer as the year progresses.

EARLY START With a little forethought, it is possible to make preparations to help get the earliest start in the garden and to overcome some of the problems caused by the low temperatures. Covering the soil with a sheet of black plastic will help to absorb the sun's heat and will make the soil beneath the plastic covering several degrees warmer than it would otherwise be, giving a head start for the plants. The most important factor is to reduce the contact between the plastic and the soil surface, to prevent the soil from becoming too wet as the condensation from the warm soil is trapped beneath the plastic. This effect can be greatly reduced by standing upturned pots at regular intervals on the soil before the plastic covering is put on. This will allow a good airflow under the cover and let the moisture escape.

For areas where vegetables are to be grown, loose-fitting fleece or white plastic can be laid over the newly emerged crop to create a warmer microclimate underneath. These "floating" mulches stretch and lift as the plants beneath them grow and can be removed once the temperatures have risen sufficiently for the plants to suffer no more checks.

Cultivation can also be used to help the soil warm up. Forking over the soil allows more warm air into it, opening up the structure to allow better penetration of natural sunlight. But beware: As the soil becomes warmer,

weed seeds will often germinate more rapidly. Cultivated soil will be much warmer in the top $2^3/_4$–3in (7–8cm) than noncultivated soil. If organic mulches are being used to warm the soil, they should be applied once the soil has begun to warm up, to trap in the heat, otherwise they will heat up while the soil below remains cold. If a manure is being used to improve the soil structure, select one based on horse or chicken waste, which produces a hot fermentation as it rots down. Only use unripened ("hot") manure on unplanted ground. It will burn and kill plants.

Where cold frames or cloches are used, either to overwinter plants that are not fully hardy or to provide protection and early growth for cuttings and seedlings needed for an early start in the garden, there are a number of methods that can be used. Incorporating a dark-colored material (such as peat or something similar) into the soil will absorb the sun's heat and help make the environment inside the frame warm up more quickly. Also, to reduce the amount of heat lost from inside the frame overnight, lay an insulating blanket of plastic bubble wrap over the glass cover each night. Remove the following morning to help reduce the fluctuations between the

day and night temperature. The advantage of using bubble wrap is that it will allow some sunlight to travel through it, so it is less important that the covering is removed very early in the morning.

UNDER COVER For plants growing in a greenhouse, sunroom, or indoors on a window sill, early spring can be a time of serious risk. Over the winter, many of these plants have gradually adapted to poor light levels, with the result that any new growth may be lush and soft, and vulnerable to sudden changes. These plants can suffer from scorching if there is a warm period with bright sunlight, even for just a couple of hours. The sun's power, when magnified by the glass windows, can even disfigure some shoots.

It may be necessary to protect these plants for the first few really bright days of spring sunshine until they adjust to the unaccustomed light levels. Move the plants out of direct sunlight or use some form of shading to filter the light and reduce the intensity during the brightest, hottest part of the day. Applying water to the floor or in trays of gravel around the base of plants will raise humidity levels and help reduce the effects of these short periods of intense sunlight. It can be harmful to apply water directly onto the leaves during these bright spells, especially if the leaves have a surface coating of hairs, as this may lead to scorching of the plant tissues.

ABOVE *Although plants may be growing slowly, even in a greenhouse, they will still need to be checked and watered regularly, especially if the winter and early spring days have been sunny.*

RIGHT *Younger plants will benefit from the protection of a cold frame, but it is important to provide some ventilation on warm days or the new growth will become too soft.*

FROST DAMAGE At temperatures fractionally below 32°F (0°C), ice begins to form inside the cells of the plant. This is not necessarily harmful, as any damage that does occur depends on the plant involved, the speed at which the temperature drops, and the age of the tissue subjected to these low temperatures. Rapid chilling of delicate young tissues can do great damage to new shoots, but the level of damage still depends on a number of factors.

The sensitive tissue of hardy plants will recover if the temperature drops slowly and steadily, as long as it also rises slowly, giving the tissue a chance to adjust to ice gradually forming inside the cells, and then changing back into water. The greatest frost damage usually occurs in late winter and early spring, when the temperature slowly drops just below freezing at night and quickly rises several degrees above freezing the following morning. This is especially so when the chilled plants are heated by warm, direct sunlight on the frozen tissues, so that in many cases the spring damage to flowers and young shoots is caused by rapid thawing rather than slow freezing.

FROST PROTECTION Damage from freezing can be greatly reduced by the formation of ice on the outside of the plant. This may occur naturally if dew forms before a night frost, as the dew will freeze before the plant's sap. If the surface of the plant is dry, the ice will form inside the plant, resulting in frost damage to young shoots and blooms. Sprinkling plants with water as an antifrost measure works because the heat lost from the water as it turns into ice helps protect the plant tissue encased within it. As the water freezes from the outside in, there may also be a layer of water between the ice and the

ABOVE LEFT AND ABOVE *Those plants that flower in the depths of winter have quite hardy flowers, while those that flower in the spring are much more vulnerable due to widely fluctuating temperatures caused by warm days and freezing-cold nights. (Left:* Scilla bifolia *'Rosea'. Right:* Cornus mas.*)*

BELOW *Evergreens, such as conifers, are damaged by wind chill rather than low temperatures. Icy winds draw moisture from the plant at a very rapid rate, injuring the foliage and turning it brown.*

plant tissue to act as extra insulation. Spraying water over the plants helps them absorb frosts as low as 23°F (-5°C) for short periods. Spraying frozen plants with water before the sun rises and warms them can help thaw the shoots slowly in a controlled way, which reduces frost damage.

Covering frozen shoots with fleece to protect them from early morning sun also allows them to warm slowly over a few hours, helping to reduce frost damage after frost of 36–7°F (2–3°C). For low-growing plants, even sheets of dry newspaper laid over them and anchored into position will prevent damage caused by a light frost. The least effective protective material to use in this situation is clear plastic film, as it will allow the soil's warmth to reradiate out into the atmosphere, making the temperature inside the structure several degrees cooler than outside.

PESTS AND DISEASES   A number of pests and diseases that attack hardy plants take advantage of their host plant to survive through winter. Mildew on apples and ornamental crab apples, peach leaf curl and spur blight on plums and cherries, and gall mites on black currants will all survive winter inside the dormant buds of plants. The problem arises as the buds open, when the new leaves develop, and the pests and diseases emerge with them to give rise to early infection of the new growth. It is worth spraying with an appropriate pesticide or fungicide as soon as the buds open, as this early control can drastically reduce the need to use more chemicals later on.

ABOVE   *Young shoots poking through the soil can be protected with a loose layer of mulch, which should be applied during the warmest part of the day to trap in some heat.*

LEFT   *As the new leaves emerge and expand from the winter buds, as with this* Prunus subhirtella, *certain types of plant pest and disease often emerge at the same time to attack this soft tissue.*

RIGHT   *To combat the risk of frost damage, some plants, such as this* Corylus avellana 'Contorta', *will have their flowers (catkins) opening in stages so that some can avoid the hard frosts.*

zonal map of the U.S. and Canada

This map shows how the countries can be divided up by minimum winter temperatures. The zones are based on the United States Department of Agriculture planting zones.

KEY TO MINIMUM TEMPERATURE RANGES

To determine if a plant will flourish in your climate, first locate your zone on the map below and then check it against the zone information (indicated by the number of snowflakes) given in the plant portraits in Chapter 4. For annuals and biennials, planting dates depend on when frosts occur: Hardy annuals can be safely sown six weeks before the last spring frost, whereas tender annuals should be sown only after all danger of frost is past.

ZONE 4 ※※※※
-30°F (-34°C) TO -20°F (-29°C)

ZONE 5 ※※※※※
-20°F (-29°C) to -10°F (-23°C)

ZONE 6 ※※※※※※
-10°F (-23°C) to 0°F (-18°C)

ZONE 7 ※※※※※※※
0°F (-18°C) to 10°F (-12°C)

ZONE 8 ※※※※※※※※
10°F (-12°C) to 20°F (-7°C)

ZONE 9 ※※※※※※※※※
20°F (-7°C) to 30°F (-1°C)

ZONE 10 ※※※※※※※※※※
30°F (-1°C) to 40°F (4°C)

Zone 11 ※※※※※※※※※※※
ABOVE 40°F (4°C)

ZONE 1 ※
BELOW -50°F (-45°C)

ZONE 2 ※※
-50°F (-45°C) to -40°F (-40°C)

ZONE 3 ※※※
-40°F (-40°C) to -30°F (-34°C)

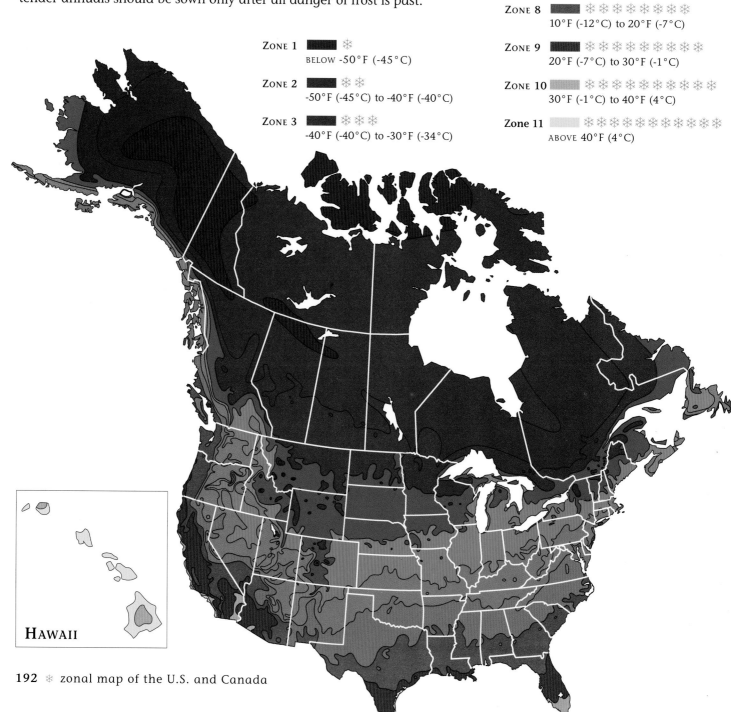

HAWAII

glossary

Abscission layer A layer of thin-walled cells that separate the point where the leaves (and fruits) are attached to the plant.

Acclimatization (acclimation) Adjusting plants to different conditions (usually cooler) than those in which they are growing.

Aerate (soil) Loosen by physical or mechanical means to allow air into the soil; for example, using a tined fork to aerate the lawn.

Alkaline A substance (soil) with a pH value of 7.0 or higher.

Alpine A plant originating from mountainous regions; often applied to a wide range of rock garden plants.

Annual A plant that completes its reproduction cycle in one year.

Apex The tip of a shoot or branch.

Aquatic Any plant that grows in water (it may be either anchored or free floating).

Axil The angle at the point where the leaf or branch joins the main stem of a plant.

Axillary bud A bud that grows in the leaf axil.

Backfill The operation of refilling a trench or hole in the ground.

Bare-rooted Plants that are offered for sale with no soil on their roots (usually grown in the field and dug up for sale).

Bark A protective layer of cells on the outer surface of the roots and stems of woody plants (*see above right*).

Basal A shoot or bud arising from the base of a plant. The basal plate is the compressed stem of a bulb.

Base dressing An application of fertilizer or organic matter incorporated into the soil prior to planting or sowing.

Bed system A system of growing vegetables in closely spaced rows to form blocks of plants, thereby reducing the area given over to paths.

Bedding plants Plants arranged in mass displays (beds) to form a colorful temporary display (*see left*).

Biennial A plant that completes its growing cycle in two growing seasons. A biennial germinates and produces roots and leaves in its first year, flowers and produces seed before dying in the second.

Biennial bearing A plant that slips into a habit of producing fruit on a two-year cycle.

Branch A shoot growing directly from the main stem of a woody plant.

Brassica A member of the cabbage family (*Cruciferae*).

Broad-leaved Deciduous or evergreen plants that have flat, broad leaves.

Bud A condensed shoot containing an embryonic shoot or flower.

Bulb A storage organ consisting of thick, fleshy leaves arranged on a compressed stem, or basal plate, found below soil level.

Calcicole A plant that prefers an alkaline, usually limy, soil (pH 7.0+).

Calcifuge A plant that prefers an acidic, usually peaty or organic, soil (pH 7.0-).

Chilling A period of low temperature (usually 36°F [2.2°C]) required by plants during dormancy to stimulate flower development.

Climber A self-supporting plant capable of growing vertically.

Cloche A small, clear (glass or plastic) portable structure used for protecting plants from extreme weather conditions.

Clone A collective term for a number of plants that have been propagated from a single individual.

Cold frame A low, clear, portable or permanent structure used for protecting and hardening-off plants.

Collar The point on the plant where i) the roots begin at the base of the main stem; ii) the swollen area where a branch joins the main stem.

Companion planting Growing certain plant combinations close together to overcome pest and disease problems organically.

Compost Well-rotted organic matter such as garden waste.

Conifer Plants that have naked ovules, often borne in cones, and narrow, needle-like foliage (*see below right*).

Coppicing The severe pruning of plants to ground level on an annual basis (see also *Stooling*).

Cordon A tree trained to produce fruiting spurs from a main stem.

Corm An underground modified stem forming a storage organ.

Crop rotation A system of moving crops in a planned cycle to improve growth and control pests and disease.

Cultivar A plant form that originated in cultivation rather than having been found growing in the wild.

Cutting A portion of a plant that is used for propagation.

Deadheading The removal of dead flower heads or seed-bearing fruits.

Deciduous Plants that produce new leaves in the spring and shed them in the fall.

Deep beds A method of growing plants (usually vegetables) in a deeply cultivated bed that has organic matter incorporated into it.

Division A method of propagation used to increase the number of plants by splitting them up into smaller units.

Dormancy A period of reduced growth through the winter.

Dormant spray The application of a fungicide/insecticide to the stems and branches of dormant deciduous plants.

Drainage The free movement of surplus water through the soil/compost.

Drill A narrow straight line in which seeds are sown.

Dry storage A method of storing edible plants in readiness for use.

Ericaceous A member of the erica family that likes acid soil conditions (see also *Calcifuge*).

Evergreen Plants that retain their growing leaves throughout the winter.

Fertile A soil rich in nutrients and biological life.

Fertilizer An organic or inorganic compound used as nutrition to help the plants grow.

Fibrous Fine, multibranched roots of a plant.

Field storage A method of storing plants (usually vegetables) in their cropping location until required.

Floating mulch A sheet of plastic or woven material that is used for protecting plants from frost. This particular type of mulch rises with the plants as they grow.

Flower The part of the plant (often highly colored) containing the reproductive organs.

Force To induce plants to start growing earlier than they usually would.

Fork A tined digging implement used for cultivating soil.

Formative pruning Pruning young plants to establish a desired plant shape and branch structure.

Framework The main permanent branch structure of a woody plant.

Frost pocket A location where cold air accumulates.

Fruit The seed-bearing vessel on a plant.

Fungicide A chemical used to control fungal disease.

Germination The process by which a seed develops into a plant.

Grafting A propagation method involving the joining of two or more separate plants together.

Greenhouse A glass- or plastic-clad structure used for growing plants under controlled (protected) conditions.

Ground cover The term used to describe low-growing, spreading plants.

Half-hardy A plant that can tolerate low temperatures, but is killed by frost.

Hardening-off Adjusting plants to different conditions (usually cooler temperatures) than those to which they are accustomed.

Hardiness zones Climatic zones graded according to the minimum annual temperature for each zone.

Hardy A plant that can tolerate the coldest temperatures where it is grown.

Harvesting The gathering or collecting of plant produce for storage or consumption.

Herbaceous A nonwoody plant with an annual top and a perennial root system or storage organ.

Hoeing A method of shallow cultivation used to kill weed seedlings.

Houseplant Tender plant that is grown indoors for decoration.

Humus The organic residue of decayed organic material.

Inorganic A man-made chemical compound (not containing carbon).

Irrigation A general term used for the application of water.

Lateral A side shoot arising from an axillary bud.

Lawn edger A tool with a semicircular cutting blade, used to trim lawn edges (often referred to as a half-moon).

Layering A propagation technique where the roots are formed on a stem before the new plant is detached from the parent plant.

Leaf The main lateral organ of a green plant (*see left*).

Leaf mold A compost-like substance that is formed from partially decomposed leaves.

Legume A member of the pea family.

Loam A soil with equal proportions of clay, sand, and silt.

Maiden A young (one-year-old) budded or grafted tree or bush.

Marginal plant A plant that prefers to grow in damp soil conditions or partially submerged in water.

Mowing Cutting down lawn grass to a required height.

Mowing strip A strip of bricks or paving slabs around the perimeter of the lawn to reduce maintenance.

Mulch A layer of material applied to cover the soil (*see right*).

Multi-row system A method of growing plants close together to regulate their overall size (also to control weeds).

Naturalize To establish bulbs or other plants so that they multiply every year and appear to have occurred naturally.

Nutrients The minerals (fertilizers) used to feed plants.

Organic Materials derived from decomposed animal or plant remains.

Outdoor storage A method of storing produce outside but with some protection; for example, by using a potato clamp.

Overwinter Keeping a plant alive through the winter, usually by protecting it from frost.

Peat Decayed sphagnum mosses or rushes and sedges.

Perennial Any plant that has a life cycle of more than three years.

pH A measure of acidity and alkalinity in a soil.

Pinching out The removal of a plant's growing point, or shoot, to encourage the development of lateral shoots.

Pollarding The severe pruning of a tree back to the main stem or trunk.

Potting on Transferring a plant to a larger container.

Propagation Techniques used to multiply one plant into a number of plants.

Propagator A structure used to propagate plants in, or a person who propagates plants.

Pruning The practice of cutting plants to improve their growth or train them to grow in a certain way.

Raised bed system A system of growing plants in beds of soil above the surrounding soil level.

Renewal pruning A pruning system based on the systematic replacement of lateral fruiting branches.

Rhizome A specialized underground stem that lies horizontally in the soil.

Root The underground support system of a plant.

Rootball The combined root system and surrounding soil of a plant.

Rootballed Plants that are dug up with the roots enclosed in a block of soil, which is held in place with burlap or a similar material (*see above*).

Sap The juice or blood of a plant.

Shoot A branch, stem, or twig.

Shrub A woody-stemmed plant (*see right*).

Sideshoot A stem arising from a branch stem or twig.

Spur A short fruit- or flower-bearing branch.

Stooling The severe pruning of plants to within 4–6in (10–15cm) of ground level on an annual basis.

Storage A method of keeping plants in an environment that delays ripening and decay.

Sublateral A sideshoot arising from an axillary bud of a lateral shoot.

Subsoil The layers of soil beneath the topsoil.

Tar oil A fungicide/insecticide applied to dormant deciduous plants.

Tender A plant that is killed or damaged by low temperatures (50ºF [-10ºC]).

Terminal bud The uppermost bud in the growing point of a stem (also known as the apical bud).

Thinning The removal of branches to improve the quality of those remaining, and to improve the overall appearance of the plant.

Tip-pruning Cutting back the growing point of a shoot to encourage the development of lateral shoots.

Top dressing An application of fertilizer or bulky organic matter that is added to the soil surface and incorporated around the base of the plant.

Topiary The practice of trimming plants into formal shapes and patterns.

Tree A woody perennial plant usually consisting of a clear stem or trunk and a framework or head of branches.

Training The practice of making plants grow into a particular shape or pattern.

Transplanting Moving plants from one growing area to another.

Tuber A root or stem modified to form a storage organ.

Variegated Plant parts (usually leaves) with two or more colors forming spots, edging, stripes, or an irregular pattern.

Wind chill A combination of low temperatures and strong winds that often causes tissue damage (cold desiccation) to plants in winter.

Wind rock The loosening of a plant's roots caused by wind.

Wound Any cut or damaged area on a plant. Wound paint is a paint or paste applied to this area.

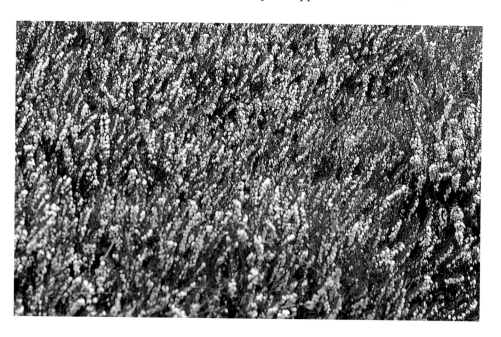

index

Page numbers in *italic* refer to illustrations.

acknowledgments

Steven Bradley "In putting this book together, I would like to thank my wife Val Bradley for her contribution to text and editing, Iain MacGregor for commissioning me to write it in the first place, and everyone at Capel Manor College for their assistance."

Marcus Harpur is very grateful to the following owners for allowing him to photograph in their gardens:
Mr. & Mrs. R. Owen, Northants; Mr. & Mrs. Geoffrey Lucas, Essex; The University Botanic Garden, Cambridge; Beth Chatto, Elmstead Market, Essex; The Savill Garden, Windsor, Berks; Hanging Gardens Nursery, Writtle, Essex; Mr. & Mrs. F. Swetenham, Essex; Mr. & Mrs. Dennis Neate, Felsted, Essex; Mr. Chris Pegden, Fingringhoe, Essex; Writtle College, Essex; Jill Cowley, Park Farm, Chelmsford, Essex; Wyken Hall, Stanton, Suffolk; Jorn Langberg, Hillwatering, Stanton, Suffolk; Mr. & Mrs. Hugh Johnson, Saling Hall, Essex; The Gardens of Little Easton Lodge, Dunmow, Essex.

The publisher would like to thank the following:
Capel Manor College, Enfield, Middlesex; Wyevale Garden Centres Plc, King's Acre Road, Hereford for the loan of tools and equipment.

 Time-Life Books is a division of Time Life Inc.

TIME LIFE INC.
Chairman and CEO	Jim Nelson
President and COO	Steven L. Janas

TIME-LIFE TRADE PUBLISHING
Vice President and Publisher	Neil Levin
Senior Director of Acquisitions and Editorial Resources	Jennifer Pearce
Director of New Product Development	Carolyn Clark
Director of Marketing	Inger Forland
Director of Trade Sales	Dana Hobson
Director of Custom Publishing	John Lalor
Director of Special Markets	Robert Lombardi
Director of Design	Kate L. McConnell

WINTER GARDENING
Project Manager	Jennie Halfant
Technical Specialist	Monika Lynde

Printed in Hong Kong by Toppan
10 9 8 7 6 5 4 3 2 1

TIME-LIFE is a trademark of Time Warner Inc. and affiliated companies.

CIP data available upon request:
Librarian, Time-Life Books
2000 Duke Street
Alexandria, Virginia 22314

ISBN 0-7370-0628-5

Books produced by Time-Life Trade Publishing are available at a special bulk discount for promotional and premium use. Custom adaptations can also be created to meet your specific marketing goals. Call 1-800-323-5255.
Every effort has been made to ensure that photography, illustrations and text are accurate at the time of going to press.